"Lance Witt understands both the dynamics of church ministry and the interior landscape of the soul. . . . In *Replenish,* he has written wise counsel, in highly readable chunks, that addresses directly and transparently those parasites that will seek to feed on a church leader's spirit."

—**John Ortberg,** author of *The Me I Want to Be*

"Like many in ministry, I've found myself drowning in techniques and tools to the neglect of my soul. It doesn't matter how you got there; it matters how you get out. Now Lance Witt has thrown you a life preserver with a perfect toss. Grab on and let him pull you back to Jesus, the only one who can replenish your soul and power your ministry."

—**Will Mancini,** author of *Church Unique;* founder of Auxano

"*Replenish* is a must-read for everyone serving in ministry. Lance not only challenges the reader to lead from a spiritually healthy place but also gives tangible steps to cultivating the healthy soul we all long for. I found myself reading through the chapters slowly, allowing the words to both minister to and challenge me. I will be taking our entire church staff through this book.

"In ministry it's easy to work so hard for God that we miss the work God wants to do in us. Lance's book is a call back to the spiritual health and order that we know we've been created for."

—**Todd Mullins,** executive pastor, Christ Fellowship, West Palm Beach, Florida

"Lance does a tremendous job of reminding us what is most important in life and ministry and calling us back to practices that restore our souls. Only from a full life and heart can we make our greatest impact for God and others. I'm thankful for Lance, who shows the way."

—**Jud Wilhite,** senior pastor, Central Christian Church, Las Vegas; author, *Eyes Wide Open*

"This book is written by a wise and seasoned fellow traveler who speaks with authority, insight, and compassion about our greatest need as leaders . . . a healthy soul. I have been privileged to watch, listen, and learn from Lance Witt as he has helped me replenish my soul. I think every leader should read this book at least once a year to recalibrate *what* we do with *how* and *why* we do it. 'For what does it profit a pastor if he grows a big ministry and loses his soul?'"

—**Chip Ingram,** senior pastor, Venture Christian Church; president, Living on the Edge Ministries

"Unfortunately, it's possible to grow your ministry and poison your soul at the same time. Lance Witt has spent more than twenty-five years in the local church and understands the dangers of ministry. *Replenish* not only identifies soul toxins but also offers a prescription for health. This is a must-read for those who want to *be* well, not just *do* well."

—**Tony Morgan,** pastor, author, consultant

"I trust Lance Witt with all my heart. Why? Because he knows how to reach into the heart of a leader and guide him/her to spiritual health. He has done that for me. Lance knows Jesus, understands people, and has unusual insight into the issues facing ministry leaders. *Replenish* should be mandatory reading for all leaders; it's a book that will care for your soul and lead you to a place of greater health."

—**Doug Fields,** speaker, author, pastor,
founder of Simply Youth Ministry

"There is no place more lonely in the world than in leadership. It brings great rewards but also great challenges to the heart of a leader. Lance Witt has written a pivotal book for the spiritual, social, and mental health of a leader. Being replenished is such an important issue in today's church. I encourage you to read this book, pray over this book, and apply its principles in your life to ensure that you are the leader God intended you to be."

—**Jonathan Falwell,** pastor, Thomas Road Baptist Church,
Lynchburg, Virginia

"Lance Witt is a pastor to pastors. I've personally benefited from his wisdom and so have those pastors in my coaching networks. Now he has made that wisdom available to us all in this highly anticipated book. If you are a pastor, get this book and let it feed your soul. If you know a pastor, honor him with the gift of this book."

—**Nelson Searcy,** lead pastor, The Journey Church of the City;
founder, *www.ChurchLeaderInsights.com*

"*Replenish* challenges church leaders not only to lead others well but also to take a hard look at their own spiritual health. With practical steps for detoxing your soul, sustaining a lifetime of spiritual health, and leading your ministry team, Lance Witt has provided leaders with a useful tool to use both individually and within their team."

—**Ed Stetzer,** coauthor of *Transformational Church*

REPLENISH

Leading From a Healthy Soul

LANCE WITT

a division of Baker Publishing Group
Grand Rapids, Michigan

© 2011 by Lance Witt

Published by Baker Books
a division of Baker Publishing Group
P.O. Box 6287, Grand Rapids, Michigan 49516-6287
www.bakerbooks.com

Printed in the United States of America

Library of Congress Cataloging-in-Publication Data

Witt, Lance.
    Replenish : leading from a healthy soul / Lance Witt.
        p.   cm.
    Includes bibliographical references.
    ISBN 978-0-8010-1354-6 (pbk. : alk. paper)   1. Clergy—Religious life.   I. Title.
    BV4011.6.W58   2011
    253′.2—dc22   2011002563

12   13   14   15   16   17   18   8   7   6   5   4   3   2

To Connie

Because of your . . .

Fun-loving personality,
Infectious laugh,
Unpretentious spirit,
Life-giving belief, and
Unshakable love,
. . . I am a better person . . . a better Christ follower.

You have been my best friend in ministry and in life.
I can't imagine my life without you.

CONTENTS

FOREWORD

Because of our tendency to romanticize Bible characters, it's a good thing periodically to look at the actual account of their lives. Eli was a colossal failure and conflict-avoider as a father. Samson was a walking impulse-control disorder. Moses was a fugitive. Elijah went through depression, suicidal ideation, exhaustion, and burnout. John the Baptist had followers disappointed that his congregation was shrinking. Paul ended up in prison.

All of which is to say I'm not sure ministry has ever been easy.

But I know for sure that people doing ministry in our day face massive challenges. And it's not just on the leadership, skill development, and missional effectiveness fronts.

We are facing soul challenges.

This past summer I went on the first sabbatical I've had in thirty years of church ministry. I was instructed by our elders to do nothing for seven weeks—no writing, no speaking, no traveling to study best-practice churches . . . nothing. I had never done so much nothing in my life, and was surprised how good I was at it.

And the greatest gift was the realization that I could be loved and free and full of life without constantly being in production mode.

One of the comments that struck me most deeply came toward the end, from a conversation with a mentor. I asked what I needed to do to help our church be effective at spiritual transformation, and this was his immediate response: "You must live with deep contentment, joy, and confidence in your experience of everyday life with God."

A pastor should be the happiest person in the church.

Lance Witt understands both the dynamics of church ministry and the interior landscape of the soul. He has worked in high-performance ministry contexts. He understands the joys and pressures of church leadership. In *Replenish* he has written wise counsel, in highly readable chunks, that address directly and transparently those parasites that will seek to feed on a church leader's spirit.

Jesus invited his followers to enter into the life of the "easy yoke." This is a hunger that never dies. I hope these words can guide you into The Way.

John Ortberg

PREFACE

Most days I love the church. But there are days when the church drives me crazy. After being in local ministry for thirty years, I understand why leaders walk away. I understand why they can be disillusioned and cynical. I understand why those who used to be filled with vision and passion are empty and filled with resentment and regret. I get it.

With the current opportunities and challenges facing us in ministry today, it is no small task to stay emotionally healthy and spiritually replenished.

When I was at Saddleback Church, I remember Rick Warren often talking about how the church's central issue was not growth but health. When churches are healthy, growth will be the natural byproduct.

But what doesn't get talked about as much is the importance

of the leader's health. We will never grow healthy churches with unhealthy leaders.

This book is all about the leader. It's not about your organizational structure, your missional strategies, or your ministry goals. It's about *you*.

Much of what you're going to read in these pages comes out of my own journey. My own drivenness and insecurity, combined with a church culture obsessed with vision and success, led to a long-term neglect of my own soul.

In recent years I have begun traveling the road to soul replenishment. I've begun to take to heart Paul's words:

> Let us cleanse ourselves from everything that can defile our body or spirit.[1]

In ministry there are many seductions that can defile our spirit and leave us spiritually unhealthy.

Getting healthy will require us to pull back the veneer. It won't happen until we're serious enough to get honest, own our stuff, and take responsibility for our soul care. We'll need to go to some of the most private corners of our soul . . . dark places where personal ambition, insecurity, fear, and brokenness reside. These and other lurking soul predators would love to devour you, those you love, and your ministry.

I've tried earnestly to be forthright about my own journey with these issues and what I am learning on the road to spiritual health.

After an introduction, this book breaks down into four sections.

- *De-Toxing Your Soul.* This opening section describes some of the soul-endangering toxins inherent in contemporary ministry.
- *Start Here . . . Start Now.* In these brief chapters you'll dis-

cover some baby steps for beginning to pay attention to your soul.

- *Sustaining a Lifetime of Health.* Here we focus on habits and practices that can build a lifetime of health. These chapters will help you learn soul care so that no matter your ministry circumstances, you can thrive spiritually and emotionally.

- *Building Healthy Teams.* This final section is about passing it on and creating a healthy leadership culture. The bridge between a healthy leader and a healthy ministry is a healthy team.

At the end of each chapter are a few questions for reflection and discussion. These could be used in conversation with a trusted friend or in discussion with your team. It's my hope that these pages will spark honest, helpful, and hopeful "soul conversations."

My greatest desire in writing this book is that it would lead you toward Jesus. May your intimacy with him transcend all of ministry's clutter and noise and busyness. And may you be reminded that your ministry is not your life . . . Jesus is.

INTRODUCTION

one

THE IDOLATRY OF LEADERSHIP

W hat's missing in the church today?" This question was posed to a well-known mega-church pastor. His one-word answer was "vision," and I couldn't disagree more with his assessment.

We are obsessed with leadership and intoxicated by vision. There's more big talk, big ideas, and big dreams than ever before. Over the last twenty-five years, vision and leadership have become the topics of choice for pastors. There has been a tidal wave of conferences, books, and podcasts devoted to helping us become better leaders. In some ministry circles, CEOs and business entrepreneurs are quoted as frequently as Scripture. Enormous energy and resources have been thrown at helping us become more effective in our pursuit of vision.

There was good reason for this.

Many of us were equipped to exegete scripture and shepherd people but ill-equipped to provide organizational leadership. As churches grew and the culture changed, pastors had to learn the world of creating budgets, managing staff, casting vision, constructing buildings, raising money, programming worship services, and managing change.

So, the inundation of leadership and church growth resources met a definite need. The focus on leadership filled a massive void, and we all have been the beneficiaries. Leadership is wonderful ... until it morphs into an idol.

It seems we have committed the same sin as the people of Israel.[1] God used a bronze serpent to bring miraculous healing, but years later it had to be destroyed because it had been turned into an idol.[2] They worshiped the provision instead of the provider.

All of the training and focus on leadership has been a gift, but we must *not* turn it into an idol. We don't need to abandon our discussion of leadership in the kingdom, but we do need to include questions that don't get enough airtime. What does spiritual leadership look like? What does healthy leadership look like? And, how should leadership in the church differ from leadership in the marketplace?

I say this because, in trying to fill the gap with leadership resources, inadvertently we have marginalized the soul side of leadership. The result is a crisis—one of spiritual health among pastors. Today's troubling statistics on pastors paint a bleak picture.

- 1,500 pastors leave the ministry permanently each month in America.
- 80% of pastors and 85% of their spouses feel discouraged in their roles.
- 70% of pastors do not have a close friend, confidant, or mentor.
- Over 50% of pastors are so discouraged they would leave the ministry if they could but have no other way of making a living.
- Over 50% of pastors' wives feel that their husband entering ministry was the most destructive thing to ever happen to their families.

- 30% of pastors said they had either been in an ongoing affair or had a one-time sexual encounter with a parishioner.
- 71% of pastors stated they were burned out, and they battle depression beyond fatigue on a weekly and even a daily basis.
- One out of every ten ministers will actually retire as a minister.[3]

We have neglected the fact that a pastor's greatest leadership tool is a healthy soul. Our concentration on skill and technique and strategy has resulted in deemphasizing the interior life. The outcome is an increasing number of men and women leading our churches who are emotionally empty and spiritually dry.

We've all witnessed the carnage of leaders who've had to leave ministry (at least for now) because of moral failure. The headlines are always about the scandalous and shocking behavior, but rarely mentioned is the back-story.

It is the story of a neglected soul and mismanaged character. Of a slow drift into relational isolation. Of being seduced by ambition. These leaders didn't intend for it to happen, but somewhere along the journey they stopped paying attention to what was going on inside of them. The shift was incremental and at times imperceptible.

Having talked to some whose ministry has come crashing down around them, I can tell you the convergence of outward success, self-deception, soul neglect, and relational isolation creates the perfect storm for disaster.

Quaker author Parker Palmer said, "A leader is a person who must take special responsibility for what's going on inside of himself or herself . . . lest the act of leadership create more harm than good."[4] We have ample evidence of Palmer's insight. When leaders neglect their interior life, they run the risk of prostituting the sacred gift of leadership. And they run the risk of being destructive instead of productive.

To further complicate this issue, those of us who serve in ministry leadership aren't very good about sending up the warning flare and letting somebody know when we're in over our heads. Revealing our struggles and asking for help can feel risky. So we try to tough it out, cover it up, and keep it in. But eventually ministry and life come unraveled.

This phenomenon is not limited to a few high-profile Christian leaders. Nor is it limited to issues of moral failure. That's just the tip of the iceberg. Pastors are leaving the ministry in record numbers. Discouragement and disillusionment are epidemic among those who lead. Obsession with numerical growth has created a generation of pastors who feel like losers. And many are choosing to fire themselves rather than fight it any longer.

Many of my pastor friends and pastors you know stand up Sunday after Sunday and faithfully preach the truth. They unselfishly minister to others and do the very best they can to lead their church. But secretly, on the inside, they are coming apart.

We may be better leaders than we used to be, but the evidence seems to say we are not better pastors or husbands or Christ followers. It is no longer safe to assume that those of us who lead in the kingdom are on track spiritually.

This reality underscores a fundamental premise of this book. When it comes to the church, you can't separate leadership from the leader. You can't divorce the message from the messenger. Yet we can become quite adept at projecting an image that does not accurately reflect what's going on inside of us.

Godly leadership is *always* inside out. God always has and always will choose to smile on men and women who are healthy, holy, and humble.

I have not been able to escape a couple of verses tucked away in Exodus 28. Here Moses records in painstaking detail about the priestly garments, with intricate instructions for making the breastpiece, the ephod, the robe, the tunic, the turban, and the sash.

But twice Moses moves beyond the externals and trappings of ministry to speak of the character and honor of the role.

> Make sacred garments for your brother Aaron to give him dignity and honor.[5]
> Make tunics, sashes and caps for Aaron's sons to give them dignity and honor.[6]

In our generation, respect and dignity certainly do not come from tunics and ephods. Nor, in my opinion, do they come from great leadership technique. In fact, I believe it is dangerous to equip church leaders with vision and leadership technique without equipping them to be spiritually healthy. True spiritual dignity comes from a healthy soul and a life marked by spiritual power and the presence of Christ.

With everything that is in me, I believe Jesus Christ is the hope of the world. And I believe the church is his plan for accomplishing his purposes on earth. It is breathtaking to ponder the possibility that the Great Commission could be completed in our generation. We have unprecedented opportunity, technology, cooperation, and resources. Never before has the church been so poised for global impact.

However, the Great Commission will not be fulfilled by human ingenuity or innovative thinking alone. This God-sized task will only be completed by Spirit-filled, spiritually healthy churches. And these churches will not be spiritually healthy unless their leaders are spiritually healthy.

It's time we went back to the basics. It's time to swing the pendulum back toward the soul and toward spiritual health.

I frequently talk to people in Christian leadership who, in moments of honest reflection, long for a different kind of ministry. Even a different kind of life. They are fatigued, emotionally drained, and struggling. They wonder, "Isn't there a better way?"

Thirty years in the trenches of local church ministry has often left me wondering the same thing. If you knew me well, you'd know I do not write these pages as the expert on soul care. In fact, many of the things I'll talk about were completely unknown to me until the last few years. I write out of my own brokenness and struggle. It is a constant battle to pursue spiritual health. So many seductive distractions surround me. But I am grateful for the path on which God has me.

I want to get to the finish line still in love with Jesus, still in love with the church, still in love with being a pastor. With my head held high, with my dignity and honor still intact, I want to look back over my shoulder and say it was worth it.

Questions for Reflection and Discussion

1. How should leadership in the church look different than leadership in the marketplace?

2. When you read troubling statistics about pastors, what is your response?

3. Parker Palmer said we have to pay attention to what's going on inside us, "lest the act of leadership do more harm than good." What are some ways in which leadership could do more harm than good?

4. How is your ministry doing at helping your leaders be spiritually healthy? What could you do better?

two

HOLE IN MY SOUL

We all have a front-stage life and a back-stage life. Front stage is the public world of ministry. It's where we're noticed, where the spotlight is on us, where people applaud and affirm us. On the front stage everything is orderly and neatly in its place. It's where we cast vision, inspire others, and lead with skill. Front stage is all about *doing.*

But we also have a back-stage life, and the two are connected. If we neglect the back stage, eventually the front stage will fall apart. While the front stage is the public world of leadership, the back stage is the private world of the leader. The back stage is private, always dark, and usually messy. The audience isn't allowed there. Back stage has no spotlight and no glory. What happens back stage facilitates and empowers what takes place on the front stage. Back stage is all about "being."

As ministry leaders, we know how to have front-stage conversations. We talk freely about attendance and strategy and services and vision and volunteers and staff. But where is the conversation about our back-stage life? Who is talking to you about you?

Back-stage conversations don't come naturally to most of us. As leaders in the kingdom we may feel a subtle pressure to have it all together. Talking honestly about the messiness of our private, interior world feels risky. It's safer to limit the conversation to the front stage. Or we may be so focused on the vision that our back stage isn't even on our radar.

When the Wesleyan bands (small groups) got together, the first thing they asked each other was a back-stage question: "How is it with your soul?" I don't know if in forty years of following Jesus anyone has ever asked me that question.

For most of my ministry I neglected my back-stage life, the care of my soul. After all, front stage is where the action is. But I am learning that the key to the Christian life is found back stage, and the only way to be healthy is to pay attention to it.

This is exactly what Jesus taught—that the Christian life is inside out, that the private informs the public. He taught that out of the overflow of the heart, the mouth speaks. He taught that the root (back stage) determines the fruit (front stage).

These chapters are dedicated to helping us pay attention to our back-stage life and begin to take steps toward an ordered and healthy soul.

A good place to start is acknowledging that many of us in leadership feel like we have a hole in our soul. Ministry drains us, sucks the life out of us, and the result is we are running on empty.

We get up to speak and deep down we know we're teaching about a life we aren't living. When ministry needs present themselves, we find ourselves not caring like we used to. Out of obligation and "doing my job," we go through the motions but our heart isn't really in it.

We have this gnawing feeling in our gut that something is missing. This isn't how it was supposed to be. We find ourselves with less joy and more frustration, less compassion and more cynicism. Some days we dream of getting out. And, if the truth were known, we're not hiding it as well as we think. Those closest to us are beginning to see it.

Imagine that your soul is like a bucket. I have learned there are two forces at work that will put holes in your bucket and drain out the life.

First, there are *external forces*. The seduction of leadership, the grind of ministry, the brokenness of our culture, and the pace of twenty-first-century life create an environment in which it's very challenging to stay healthy at the soul level. If not managed well, these factors can poke a hole in our bucket and leave us feeling empty.

As Ruth Barton writes in *Strengthening the Soul of Your Leadership*,

> It is possible to gain the world of ministry success and lose your own soul in the midst of it all.[1] . . . These days (and maybe every day) there is a real tension between what the human soul needs in order to be truly well and what life in leadership encourages and even requires.[2]

It's scary to realize that the path to external success and internal emptiness can be the same road.

Furthermore, there are *internal forces* at work. Part of the problem is we're poking holes in our bucket from the inside as a result of insecurities, broken places, and compulsions.

Again, not all of the dangers to my soul are external pressures. Beyond the drain of contemporary ministry, all of us have a shadow side to our leadership. Insecurities, broken places, and secret sin can leave us empty.

In the excellent work *Overcoming the Dark Side of Leadership*, Sam Rima talks about internal brokenness that led to an unhealthy soul.

> I slowly began to realize that paradoxically the personality traits and inner drives that brought me success as a leader were also what had ultimately caused desperation.[3]

That's why it's so important to learn the art of soul care. For some of us, simply acknowledging we have a soul that needs to be cared for is the first step. Most days as a pastor I didn't give much thought to the fact that I had a soul. Your soul is the invisible, eternal part of you. It's the real you. If you lose part of your body or have an organ transplant, it doesn't change your soul. Your hair may turn gray (or, as in my case, turn loose), you may get wrinkles or put on twenty pounds, but you are still you.

Our soul is far and away the most valuable possession we have. Just as you need to tend to your body to be physically healthy, you must tend to your soul if you want to be spiritually healthy.

There is hope. Despite the challenges of leadership in our generation, it is possible to have a healthy soul and a dynamic, impacting ministry. I would like to suggest a three-part strategy this book will guide you through.

- *Realize.* This is about taking the time to reflect and be honest about the issues that are a threat to your soul. Part of the process will be to discover, identify, and name the things putting holes in your bucket.
- *Repair.* Once you've identified the holes, you can start to take steps to repair them. The section of this book called "Start Here . . . Start Now" is intended to help you start taking some steps toward a healthier soul.
- *Refill.* Once you've been forthright about what's threatening your soul and have begun to patch the holes, you can begin to focus on refilling your bucket. This is about learning to fill your soul and lead from a healthy place. You'll discover some habits that can sustain a lifetime of spiritual health. By the way, this has everything to do with your ministry effectiveness. As Mother Teresa said, "To keep a lamp burning, we have to put oil in it."

Henri Nouwen painted a picture of leaders with a healthy soul:

> The central question is, Are the leaders of the future truly men and women of God, people with an ardent desire to dwell in God's presence, to listen to God's voice, to look at God's beauty, to touch God's incarnate Word and to taste fully God's infinite goodness? [4]

That's the kind of leader I want to be.

Questions for Reflection and Discussion

1. How well does your team engage in back-stage conversations? How well do you personally engage in back-stage conversations?

2. Who in your life has been helpful with your back stage? How has that relationship been helpful?

3. If someone asked you today, "How is it with your soul?" what would you say?

4. What in ministry most pokes holes in your bucket and drains your soul? What steps could you take to keep this from happening?

three

YOUR MINISTRY IS NOT YOUR LIFE

Paul said, "When Christ, who is your life, appears, then you also will appear with him in glory."[1] Notice the words "Christ, who is your life." *Jesus is my life.* He is the center of my universe; everything revolves around my relationship with him. My whole life has been surrendered to him as my King and Lord.

I was crystal clear about this when I went into ministry as a young man. But there certainly have been seasons through the years when I lost that clarity. My ministry became my identity. My ministry became my first love. My ministry consumed all my spiritual passion. My ministry (not Jesus) was my life. The unintended byproduct during those seasons was a slow disconnect from Jesus.

When this happens, you begin to do ministry in the flesh. You begin to think serving God is all about working hard, being strategic, developing leaders and executing vision. You fundamentally begin to believe that it's up to you.

When you have disconnected from the Vine (Jesus), ministry will become joyless striving and stressful pushing. It will become a hassle and a burden. This is what happened to the priests in

Malachi; the whole book, a response to spiritual drift, is four chapters of rebuke.

In chapters 2 and 3, the Lord rebukes the people (the congregation) for their disobedience. In the opening chapter, though, God's rebuke is directed toward the priests, the professional ministers. What was happening in the congregation was a byproduct of what was happening in the leadership. God was not pleased with their offerings or with the attitude of their service in ministry.

> *"You say, 'What a burden!' and you sniff at it contemptuously,"* says the LORD Almighty.[2]

Carrying out the duties and responsibilities of ministry had become not a blessing but an annoyance. As a result, the leaders began to despise their calling. Serving wasn't a blessing, it was a burden. Ministry wasn't an honor, it was a hassle.

This is a good picture of what happens to us when we get disconnected from Jesus.

Moses' life serves as a good example for ministry leadership.

When God came to Moses and gave him the assignment of leading his people, Moses had a predictable response: "Who am I, that I should go to Pharaoh and bring the Israelites out of Egypt?"[3]

God essentially replied, *They will follow you because you have my presence in your life. That is what qualifies you for spiritual leadership.* It wasn't because Moses was the brightest, or most skilled, or most winsome. The one characteristic that would give his leadership credibility and spiritual power was God's presence.

That wasn't enough for Moses—he wanted something more tangible, more dazzling.

Fast forward to Sinai. Moses has led the people out of Egypt and is up on the mountain with God, receiving the Ten Commandments.

> The tablets were the work of God; the writing was the writing of God, engraved on the tablets.[4]

Imagine this unbelievable scene. In this moment, Moses is in the very presence of God, who is literally etching the law into stone.

Down below, however, the people are making an idol. What a contrast to what's happening on the mountaintop. God is so furious he wants to wipe them out; Moses intercedes, and God backs down. He will send them into the Promised Land, with one caveat. God will send an angel to accompany them; *his* presence won't go with them.

> I will not go with you, because you are a stiff-necked people and I might destroy you on the way.[5]

Moses' response gives us some hints about how far his relationship with God has developed over the years. He has matured, and his soul is deeply connected to God.

> *If your Presence does not go with us, do not send us up from here.*[6]

In Exodus 3, God's presence wasn't enough for Moses; he needed the dramatic and spectacular. In Exodus 33, God's presence was all that mattered to him. Later the Bible says of Moses that he had a face to face relationship with God.[7]

I want that.

God was Moses' life. He had learned the valuable lesson that relationship comes before responsibility.

If we back up a couple of verses we can hear Moses tell God what he needs for the leadership task ahead. His request might surprise you.

> You have been telling me, "Lead these people," but you have not let me know whom you will send with me. You have said, "I know you by name and you have found favor with me." If you are pleased with me, teach me your ways so I may know you and continue to find favor with you. Remember that this nation is your people.[8]

Moses doesn't ask for skill or charisma. He says, "Teach me your ways so I may know you." *It's all about relationship.* The relationship would give him the strength to carry out the responsibility.

This is exactly what Jesus taught us.

I am the vine; you are the branches. Those who remain in me, and I in them, will produce much fruit. For apart from me you can do nothing.[9]

"Remaining" is all about relationship. It's about making Jesus your life and then letting the ministry flow out of that relationship. The apostle Paul says it a little differently: "The Kingdom of God is not just a lot of talk; it is living by God's power."[10]

As ministry leaders, we have been called to do a hard thing. We are kingdom bringers to a dark world. The battle is real. Add to this that we are broken and frail and flawed. We desperately need the life of Jesus flowing through us in order to carry out our kingdom calling.

That's why it's imperative for us to pay attention to our souls.

Jesus is an incredible gift to us. And as people in ministry we get the privilege of carrying that gift to the world. Our ministry can be likened to the box and wrapping paper and bow. Our size and style of wrapping paper and boxes can vary from ministry to ministry, but we're all trying to deliver the same gift.

Never lose sight of the fact that the box (your ministry) is not as valuable as the gift (Jesus). And the only reason the box exists is to deliver the gift. You have dedicated your life to the gift, not to the box.

Questions for Discussion and Reflection

1. Share a little from your story of how you came to know and follow Jesus.

2. Share about a time or season when ministry felt like a burden. For you personally, when ministry becomes a burden, what are the signs?

3. How do you know when you are living in God's power?

4. What are some ways you can keep the focus on the "gift" instead of the "box"?

DE-TOXING YOUR SOUL

four

IMAGE MANAGEMENT

mage management. There's nothing particularly wrong with those two words, but when you put them together and give them to a ministry leader, it is a deadly cocktail. Image management is what we begin to do when our inner world becomes separated from our outer world.

If the outward and inward are not integrated, we literally come apart. And we have seen plenty of examples in recent years of leaders whose lives have disintegrated.

Because Jesus knew the dangers of disintegration, he had zero tolerance for duplicity. He railed more against image management than anything else he talked about and didn't pull any punches when talking about the image management of the Pharisees.

> Everything they do is for show. On their arms they wear extra wide prayer boxes with Scripture verses inside, and they wear robes with extra long tassels.[1]

To the average synagogue attendee, these ministry professionals looked zealous and committed. Prayer boxes, tassels, and tithes were their trappings, but the problem was not the trappings—these could be legitimate expressions of spiritual devotion. The problem was the Pharisees used them to project the image of a life they had stopped living.

According to Jesus, the Pharisees seemed clean, righteous, and pure, but inwardly they were filthy, impure, and self-indulgent. Paying attention to your outer life while your inner life languishes is like getting a facelift when you have a malignant tumor.

If you've been in ministry any length of time, you know what it is to be a Pharisee. We all know what it's like to prop up an external image that doesn't match our soul reality. Sometimes the life I preached about on Sunday wasn't the life I was experiencing Monday to Saturday.

The greatest danger, really, isn't in projecting a false image; there's a Pharisee inside all of us, and I suspect we'll struggle with this as long as we live. The greatest danger is in getting comfortable with it, learning how to "succeed" with a disconnected soul. Over time we can become very adept at playing the image-management game. The truth is you don't have to have a healthy soul to be seen as a success in ministry.

You are walking in a ministry minefield when your outward success begins to outpace your inward life. In recent years we've seen people whose outward success was beyond what their character could handle. Part of what makes this so challenging is that outward success brings strokes and affirmation and applause. It's easy to put energy in the areas where I feel significant and important.

In the movie *Avatar*, Marine Jake Sully is a paraplegic whose military assignment is to gather intel by using an "avatar" identity. Even though he was broken, the avatar he lived through virtually was strong, powerful, and whole. The avatar everyone saw was radically different than the Jake Sully no one saw. Many of us in ministry feel the need to assume an "avatar" identity.

A Latin phrase on an ancient coat of arms speaks to the tension of image management. *Esse quam videri* means "to be rather than appear to be," and those words resonate with my spirit. I don't want there to be a gap between what I am and what I portray. I don't want to project an avatar when my internal world is broken. But as the years go by, I have found it easy to function out of my experience and gifting and skill rather than dependence upon God.

Many years ago I lived in Dallas and worked downtown. At the time, downtown Dallas was undergoing a major facelift.

Across the street from the old historic First Baptist Church was a dilapidated, boarded-up YMCA building. We heard it had been purchased and that a skyscraper was going in its place. Weeks went by and nothing happened. We'd see an occasional worker go in or come out, but nothing changed. No crews, no machinery, no wrecking ball.

Then we were notified that on a Saturday morning the old building was coming down, so we went downtown to watch. At the appointed time, we heard a muffled explosion. Slowly the walls began to crack, bricks began to crumble, and finally the whole thing fell in on itself in a pile of dust and rubble.

All those weeks when we thought nothing was going on, when nothing was changing on the outside, a systematic dismantling was taking place inside. Weaknesses were being exposed, and skilled demolition experts were working their magic. The end result was a total collapse, an implosion.

This image has served as a warning to me. When I practice image management I am headed toward an implosion.

I remember sitting in Milwaukee a few years back with a group of veteran Christian leaders, talking about spiritual formation. One white-haired man at the table was probably in his upper sixties and had served in ministry with InterVarsity more than forty years. I will never forget the words that quietly but powerfully rolled off his lips: "The older I get, the less concern I have with what I have or have not done and the more concern I have for what I have or have not become."

The older I get, the more his words ring true to me. They're a call to pay attention to what's happening inside. They are a reminder that I have a soul. I am more than simply what I achieve outwardly.

A healthy soul keeps my life glued together (integrated). Neglect of the soul and preoccupation with doing, achieving, and succeeding will inevitably lead to image management.

So, how are you doing with this one? If your life were a building, are you being dismantled from the inside? Is an implosion in your future? Take a risk this week and get together with a trusted friend. Have a gut-level conversation about image management.

Questions for Discussion and Reflection

1. What are some signs when someone's outward and inward lives aren't integrated?

2. What is one area of gifting where you could be tempted to lead out of skill and not dependence on God?

3. When are you most vulnerable to propping up an external image that doesn't match your internal world?

4. When you read the following statement, what thoughts and feelings are stirred in you? "The older I get, the less concern I have with what I have or have not done and the more concern I have for what I have or have not become."

five

SEDUCTION OF AMBITION

A mbition is a double-edged sword. When it is God-directed and Spirit-managed, it can bear tremendous fruit. When it is restrained by humility, ambition can be a powerful motivator. But when it is hijacked by self and ego, it can leave a wake of destruction in its path.

I have wrestled with this issue for most of my life. If you have leadership gifts, you know what it is to be captivated by vision. You know what it is to have dreams of what could be. You know what it is to want to do something significant with your life.

Here's where it gets sticky.

Is this drive and desire and motivation about me or about God and his purposes? If we're honest, we would have to admit that our hearts are entangled with God-directed motives and self-directed motives. Sorting them out is complex. A discussion of motives and ambition takes us to an inner place that's hidden from everyone. Part of what makes ambition so dangerous is that it resides in the unseen world of the soul. This unseen part of your life is actually a very powerful force.

God wired into every one of us a creative tension. On the one hand, we have what the ancients referred to as a "fire in the belly." This is our inner source of vision, our longing to make a difference, our will to achieve. In recent years in the ministry world we have been pouring gasoline on these fires. Well-intentioned desires to stoke the fires of godly ambition have sometimes been hijacked by personal ambition.

At the same time, God also has hardwired into us the need for quiet, solitude, rest, and reflection (a healthy soul). This is one reason God established the Sabbath: to teach us there is a healthy rhythm of life. I like to refer to this part of us as a "spiritual recliner." It's a place of rest and peace. It's more about being than doing.

You need both a fire in the belly and a spiritual recliner to be healthy. In fact, you *must* have both. Catholic author Ronald Rolheiser illustrates how the two work together:

> A healthy soul must do two things for us. First, it must put some fire in our veins, keep us energized, vibrant, living with zest and full of hope as we sense that life is, ultimately beautiful and worth living. . . . Second, a healthy soul has to keep us fixed together. It has to continually give us a sense of who we are, where we came from, where we are going, and what sense there is in all of this.[1]

The problem is that these two realities create strain in our lives.

> We want to be innocent and pure, but we also want to be experienced and taste all of life. . . . We want to have the depth afforded by solitude, but we also do not want to miss anything; we want to pray, but we also want to watch television, read, talk to friends, and go out. Small wonder life is often a trying enterprise and we are often tired and pathologically overextended.[2]

Think of it like this. Imagine fire in the belly (ambition) is like raw electricity. It's alive, energetic, powerful, exciting, and full of potential, but it can also be dangerous and potentially fatal. Then think of a healthy soul as a transformer. A transformer serves to regulate, channel, direct, and control electricity. A transformer takes what's potentially harmful and deadly and turns it into something useful and helpful.

It seems to me we are reaping the results of a generation in the church where it has been all about raw electricity. The outcome has been a spike in leaders who are coming unglued. I have a growing conviction that it's dangerous to equip young leaders with vision, leadership, strategy, and church growth principles without equipping them to have healthy souls. We need to be just as serious about building transformers as we are about generating raw electricity.

My first pastorate was in a rural Baptist church in Arkansas. We were a small church of less than a hundred in a small town that had been the same size for a generation or more. I came out of seminary with lots of ambition and drive. Why couldn't we be the first mega-church in a town of three thousand?

But all my ambition and hard work didn't translate into much growth. I remember going to denominational meetings or occasionally running into a classmate from seminary. I dreaded those conversations because I knew the drill. Sooner or later (usually sooner) we would get to the "How are things going at your church?" question. I would try to change the subject as soon as possible. I always walked away feeling inadequate and discouraged.

The emotion and the pressure were mostly self-imposed. The emotions I felt had to do with my own ambition. In my mind the only successful pastor was the pastor of a fast-growing church. Our obsession with size and church growth has set up a generation of pastors who feel like failures.

Now, let me reveal the other side of my struggle with ambition. Fast-forward a few years to a time when I was pastoring a church that was the talk of the town. All indicators were up and to the right. By everyone's measuring stick we were a success.

Unlike before, I found myself anxious to talk to other pastors. I couldn't wait to get to the "How are things going at your church?" question. I'm ashamed to admit this, but I would find myself in a conversation looking for a way to turn and manipulate it so that I could talk about our church.

This was a whole different set of emotions than what I experienced in my small, rural church in Arkansas, but it was nonetheless related to ambition. The truth is that success opens doors and creates opportunities, yet it can also lead us badly astray.

> Fire tests the purity of silver and gold, but a person is tested by being praised.[3]

Success can be just as challenging a test as failure.

I'm not quite sure when, but somewhere along the way, the measuring stick for what it means to be an effective pastor got switched. My concern is that the measuring stick of size alone can fuel a kind of ambition that is destructive.

If there is one thing I've learned in recent years, it's this: numerical growth alone is no indicator of God's favor or godly leadership. I know of pastors whose churches were growing at a double-digit pace annually when they were involved in a full-blown sexual affair. Where do we put that in our theology?

In the introduction to *Purpose-Driven Church*, Rick Warren talks about catching spiritual waves. It is God who creates waves and movements of his Spirit. We don't get to decide when the wave comes, where it comes, or how big it will be. But it's our privilege to ride a great wave and participate in what God is doing.

My fear is that Christian leaders will no longer stand on the shore looking for and praying for a wave of God's Spirit. When ambition does not have a healthy soul attached to it, we can start trying to create waves ourselves.

Questions for Discussion and Reflection

1. What is godly ambition? How is that different from personal ambition?

2. God wired us to have both a "fire in the belly" and a healthy soul ("spiritual recliner"). Which one gets the most attention in your life? What can you do to bring greater balance?

3. Solomon said that *fire tests the purity of silver and gold, but a person is tested by being praised.* Think of a time when success or achievement has been a test for you personally.

4. How can you be proactive to make sure personal ambition doesn't hijack what God is doing in your ministry or church?

six

AMBITION AMBUSH

What makes selfish ambition so insidious is we can see it in others but not in ourselves. Either because of denial or self-deception, we are usually the last person to see the unhealthy ambition that has taken root in our soul. Long before it becomes apparent to us, it is seen clearly by others.

Fénelon, the French author, said, "We have an amazing ability to self-deceive. Your self-interest hides in a million clever disguises."[1] Thomas Kelly said it even more colorfully: "O how slick and weasel-like is self-pride."[2]

When you've been in ministry leadership awhile, you learn how to cloak ambition in kingdom language. You can wrap ambition in God talk and sanctify it.

This is one reason it's so important to build solitude into your life. At least for me, during times of listening and quiet God turns the spotlight of the Holy Spirit onto my ambition. But if I'm moving at an insane pace and there is no room in my life for quiet, I will miss God's voice. And I will continue on a path of self-deception.

Many years ago my wife and I watched an old suspense thriller,

There's a Stranger in the House, about a killer targeting young college girls in a sorority. Police dispatch an all-out manhunt to find the murderer. Ultimately they trace him through a phone call made inside the house! While they were combing the entire city, he was living in the attic and wreaking havoc from within.

I have made a sobering discovery in recent years: Ambition lives in the attic of my soul. Over the last few years the Spirit has spotlighted the sin of selfish ambition and exposed it. And, it's one thing to expose it; it's another to extinguish it.

In my journey, I have learned that selfish ambition does not stay inside the soul—it leaks out. It takes on many ugly faces, *"for wherever there is jealousy and selfish ambition, there you will find disorder and evil of every kind."*[3] The apostle James is right: Wherever ambition is disconnected from a healthy soul, you will find disorder and every kind of evil. I just wonder how many problems and divisions and fights and splits in local churches could be traced back to selfish ambition.

There was a time when the fires in Southern California came dangerously close to our house. As they rapidly advanced over the hilltops, the community made every effort to create a fire break. Crews removed every piece of dry brush from yards that backed up to the wilderness area. Helicopters were in the air around the clock dumping huge buckets of water around the perimeter. Our neighborhood was spared.

The local news referred to our plight as the "perfect storm of fires." These conditions created the environment for hundreds of explosive fires. Three dangerous conditions converged: extended drought, excessive heat, and strong Santa Ana winds.

In ministry, the perfect storm for a personal disaster is also the convergence of three elements: ambition, isolation, and self-deception.

We desperately need to stare this in the face. As Fénelon said, "You ask for a cure to get well. You do not need to be cured, but killed."[4] When it comes to the deception of ambition, it doesn't need to be cured; it needs to be killed.

We need to start asking ourselves some hard and penetrating questions. We must dig beneath the surface and extract the roots that keep producing dysfunction. *Why am I so driven? Why do I keep pushing so hard? Am I obsessed with success? Do I have God's measuring stick for success? Do I have a utilitarian view of people? How has my drive to succeed hurt my family?*

So, how do you start to turn the corner? How do you begin to move away from ambition and toward humility?

The starting place is to have an accurate understanding of humility. Humility is not being down on yourself. It is not self-ridicule. I like Andrew Murray's definition.

> *It is the displacement of self by the enthronement of God. Where God is all, self is nothing.*[5]

It's interesting to study the life of Jesus and discover how many times he used the word "not" or "nothing" in reference to himself. In John, he makes statements like "in myself, I can do *nothing*" or "I do *not* please myself" or "I do *not* accept praise from men" or "I came down from heaven *not* to do my will" or "I do *nothing* on my own" or "I am *not* seeking glory for myself."

Even as the Son of God, he was aware he was not pursuing his own agenda but fulfilling the Father's plan. How incredibly humble for the infinite and perfect Son of God to say, "I'm not seeking my own glory." He lived out of a deep center of abiding connection with his Father, and as a result his "spiritual transformer" was firmly in place.

A few years ago I had the opportunity to visit the Yoido Full Gospel Church in Seoul, Korea, where Dr. David Cho is pastor. After the morning service I attended a reception where the church's vision and values were articulated. Dr. Cho described the church as a three-legged stool and said if any leg were removed, the stool would collapse.

The first two he mentioned didn't surprise me: prayer and small groups. Cho's church is renowned for its prayer ministry and thousands of cell groups. The third leg did surprise me: It wasn't biblical teaching or powerful worship or social ministry or personal evangelism. The third leg of the stool he referred to as "touch not the glory."

Cho explained that one of their core priorities was not to take any glory for themselves that rightfully belonged to God. It might not be a bad idea for those of us who lead in the church to have a "touch not the glory" covenant with our team.

> *All of you, serve each other in humility, for "God opposes the proud, but favors the humble." So humble yourselves under the mighty power of God, and at the right time he will lift you up in honor.*[6]

It is our job to humble ourselves and leave it to God when and how he honors us.

Questions for Discussion and Reflection

1. What is meant by the statement, "When you've been in ministry leadership awhile, you learn how to cloak ambition in kingdom language. You can wrap ambition in God talk and sanctify it"? Give some examples.

2. What helps you discern God-motives from self-motives?

3. James says, *Wherever there is jealousy and selfish ambition, there you will find disorder and every kind of evil.* How does selfish ambition foster disorder and evil in a ministry context?

4. How do you have godly ambition and true humility?

seven

APPROVAL ADDICTION

It's one of those moments permanently etched in my memory. On Monday nights in our small church (my first pastorate) we had a men's prayer meeting. It was a time to pray for church and community needs, and for eight to ten men to get together and talk about life.

On that particular Monday night, after we prayed, the conversation turned to another Baptist church in the area. We began to talk about their need for a pastor. Then, in passing, one of the men said, "Wouldn't it be great to have the job of a pastor? Now, that would be the easy life." Everybody laughed, and we moved on. The man who made the comment was a good man, and I know he didn't mean anything by it. It was good-natured banter.

That was more than twenty-five years ago, but to this day I remember word-for-word my internal response. *I'll show you. I'll work harder than any pastor you've ever had. You won't ever accuse me of being lazy.*

And I did show them. I worked hard and made sure I did everything I could to win their approval. Even in that rural community, I adopted a workaholic lifestyle because of something that was broken inside of me. My family and my soul paid the biggest price.

Back then I would have attributed my behavior to a commitment to Jesus and my calling to ministry. And I was sincerely and authentically devoted to Christ. But that wasn't the whole story. I also harbored an addiction to approval that has been a big part of my story.

Actually, as I ponder it now, it was more than approval I was after. I also wanted applause. I wanted to be successful and for people to know it and acknowledge it. Applause was the fuel necessary for me to feel significant.

Whether you use the word *approval* or *applause*, here's the bottom line. I was living for people and finding my worth, value, significance, and identity in what others thought of me.

When approval is a driving force in your life, it messes with your motives. You run decisions through the filter of "What will people think?" rather than "What's the right thing to do?" As a leader, I know it matters what others think, but it's not the only thing that matters. At best this filter will cloud my ability to make good and godly decisions. At worst, I can actually compromise my integrity to make sure I have approval or applause.

Approval addiction not only will mess with your motives, it also will hijack your time and emotional energy. On one side I spent too much emotional energy seeking after people's affirmation. On the other I spent way too much emotional energy worrying about criticism.

It has been said that for those of us in ministry, compliments are written in sand, but criticism is written in wet cement. That has certainly been true for me. I have carried disapproval deeply, and it takes a long time to wear off. As a result, you can end up working hard at being a diplomat and constantly sharpening your people skills to minimize criticism.

E-mail has brought a whole new challenge for approval addicts.

Now people can drop a bomb of electronic criticism they would never drop in person. The dawn of the internet has increased both the frequency and intensity of the criticism coming our way.

A reporter once asked an insightful question when interviewing a woman from the Boston Philharmonic Orchestra: "How does it feel to get a standing ovation from the crowd at the end of your performance and then wake up in the morning to a negative review in the newspaper?" Her response was even more insightful. She said over time she has learned not to pay attention to the applause of the crowd or the disapproval of the critics. She was only after the approval of her conductor. After all, he was the only person who really knew how she was supposed to perform.

When I made the decision to leave my position at Saddleback, my approval addiction fought me every step of the way.

I remember when I first joined the staff and my first set of business cards was printed. One of the other pastors picked up one off my desk, held it up, and, with tongue in cheek, said, "This card will open a lot of doors, but don't forget that the most important name on it is not yours."

He was right. People who wouldn't take my phone calls before would talk to me now because I had Saddleback Church on my card.

Resigning my position was the hardest ministry decision I've ever had to make. It is a hard place to leave; it's a great church in a great place to live. Being at such a place provides tons of ministry opportunity and platform.

As I entertained the thought of leaving, questions driven by insecurity began to consume my mind. *Will I still be asked to speak at conferences? Will people care what I have to say anymore? Will people stop answering my e-mails? Will my legacy be that of a "former" executive pastor at Saddleback?*

Over a period of about six months, I had a lot of agonizing conversations with God and with my wife. I knew this was a defining moment in my spiritual journey. And it was a lot about my willingness to surrender my need for approval and applause.

During those days God reminded me that my significance has nothing to do with the name of the church on my business card. God also drilled into my spirit that he's the conductor of the symphony; my job was to play my part and look only for his approval. At the end of the day, he will evaluate my life not on the world's definition of success but on his definition of faithfulness.

Questions for Discussion and Reflection

1. When you were growing up, how did you get approval in your family?

2. How can the desire for approval change your motives?

3. How well do you handle criticism? Are you able to let go of it and move on, or does it gnaw at you for a long time?

4. In your life, how has your desire for approval revealed itself? How much do you still struggle with this today?

eight

ISOLATION TRAP

For some reason expanded leadership influence often goes hand in hand with increased relational isolation.

I remember talking with a prominent pastor after he had to leave his church because of a lengthy affair. While he was living a double life the church was experiencing rapid growth. He told me he'd been isolated for a long time and "stiff-armed" anybody who tried to get close. He did not allow anyone to see his private world, much less speak into it. Even when people began to suspect something was going on, the lack of relationship caused them to sit and watch.

After the fact, several people told me they saw troubling signs but just didn't have the courage to confront the pastor. The church handled this explosion about as well as any I have ever witnessed. There was grace and kindness and forgiveness. But the ripples of the emotional, personal, family, and church devastation are still being felt.

Ministry is a character profession. I can't separate my private life from my public leadership. According to Jesus, it is the holiness of my private life that gives spiritual power and validation to my public ministry. This raises the stakes for my personal integrity; I must have people in my life who help me stay on track in my private world.

John Maxwell was right: "People who lead themselves well know a secret; they can't trust themselves."[1] I know from experience I can easily be self-deceived.

This reality makes one of the current ministry trends even more troubling and dangerous. With the dawn of the twenty-first century came a new focus on church planting. For many young (and some not so young) church planters the challenge and sacrifice of starting something new was more appealing than trying to transition old wineskins (structures and methods). Many pastors have watched their friends end up in a leadership straightjacket because of cumbersome governance structures.

I remember sitting in a roundtable discussion with about thirty pastors in the Kansas City area, talking about Saddleback and some recent changes we'd made to our services and ministries. One pastor spoke up: "We would love to do what you're talking about, but the truth is, most of us in this room are not really the leaders in our churches. Our formal structures and informal politics don't give us the authority to implement this kind of change." As I looked around, I saw a lot of heads nodding in affirmation of his analysis.

Many church-planting pioneers have opted to start a church and create their own problems rather than inherit problems like the ones facing those pastors.

Here's the rub. In an attempt to create structures that allow greater leadership freedom (which is a good thing), many have opted for structures that include little formal accountability (which is a bad thing). Instead of a church model where the leader answers to everyone, some have created a leadership model where they answer to no one.

It's a recipe for dysfunction and disaster when a leader is organizationally and relationally isolated. My observation is that a leader who is isolated organizationally is twice as isolated relationally.

It is slower to lead with a group, but it's also healthier and wiser. The Bible repeatedly highlights the virtue of collective wisdom. For instance:

> Without wise leadership, a nation falls; there is safety in having many advisers.[2]

I need "many advisers" because I have blind spots. I need many advisers because of my insecurities. I need many advisers because I can be self-serving. I need many advisers because I am only a part of the body, not the whole body.

These realities are not only true organizationally, they also are true privately. I need people who love me enough to protect me from myself. They love me too much to let me hurt myself and others. But the only way they will honestly show up with the hard stuff in my life is if I aggressively embrace it. Even strong people are often reticent to challenge those in positions of spiritual leadership.

I need to invest the time and build mutual trust in an accountability relationship. It is a sacred trust to give someone that kind of access to my life, and I'm not going to quickly give them the password into my private world.

One Saturday morning after I finished teaching the membership class, a new attendee came up and was a little disappointed Rick Warren wasn't there in person to teach. He went on to say he was excited to be at Saddleback, and he wanted to know if I would give him Pastor Rick's cell phone number. He said he felt called to be Rick's accountability partner and wanted to call about when the two of them could meet.

Anybody who volunteers to keep you accountable probably isn't the right person for the job. I want someone who's a bit reluctant to play that role in my life. If it's the right kind of friend, I will not only need to give permission but also a sense of responsibility. I need to look them in the eye and say, "Too much is at stake for you to be silent when you think I'm messing up. I need you to call me out."

A question I often ask people in ministry is, "Who in your life can rebuke you?" Solomon said, "He who listens to a life-giving rebuke will be at home among the wise."[3] When's the last time a trusted confidant rebuked you about how you treated someone, or an off-color joke you told, or your insensitivity to your spouse, or your distortion of the truth, or your harshness toward a team member?

A rebuke can be life-giving in the same way that a doctor exposing and removing cancer is life-giving. There's temporary pain but long-term gain. Usually when we think of rebuke, we attach words like *shame*, *guilt*, and *failure*. But a well-placed rebuke from a well-trusted friend actually exposes the stuff in my life that could destroy me. If I have a friend who loves me enough to rebuke me, it is a gift.

One more verse: "An honest answer is like a kiss of friendship."[4] It's an incredible gift to have a handful of people in my life who love me enough to tell me what I need to hear, not just what I want to hear.

Questions for Discussion and Reflection

1. Do you agree that "expanded leadership influence often goes hand in hand with increased relational isolation"? If so, what could be some reasons for this?

2. Proverbs 11:14 says that *without wise leadership, a nation falls; there is safety in having many advisers.* How are you personally and your ministry organization doing at having "many advisers"?

3. Do you have appropriate accountability in your life? Practically speaking, what would it look like for you to be more accountable?

4. Solomon said, *He who listens to a life-giving rebuke will be at home among the wise.* How can a rebuke be life-giving?

NEED FOR SPEED

I n 2010, millions and millions of Toyota vehicles were recalled due to accelerator concerns. Toyota, apart from the costs of fixing the issue, will pay out billions of dollars to settle class action suits. They've had a massive "accelerator problem," and so do people in ministry.

Many of us live with a stuck accelerator. The frantic pace of life resides in the church as much as in the community. And we have no trouble rationalizing our velocity. After all, time is short, and we're going fast for Jesus. We have been scammed into believing that an insane pace is simply the price tag of effective leadership.

This addiction to speed is pervasive. Filling up every second and compressing time characterizes our generation.

> Our ability to work fast and play fast gives us power. It
> thrills us. If we have learned the name of just one hormone,
> it is adrenaline. No wonder we call sudden exhilaration a
> "rush."[1]

We keep the pedal to the metal, trying to grab every possible opportunity. Adrenaline is our hormone of choice.

I am a hurrier. I wish I had a dollar for every time my family heard me say "hurry up." Sometimes I walk in a hurry and leave my wife behind.

But worse than my hurried step is my hurried spirit. When I have to wait, or get delayed, or a movie drags, or there is dead time in a worship service, or someone in my small group is telling a long story, I find myself internally saying *hurry up*.

I've been thinking about starting a support group for compulsive hurriers. The upside is our meetings wouldn't last long.

Hurry is more about what's going on inside you than what is going on around you. As I heard John Ortberg say once, "Hurry is not about a disordered schedule, it is about a disordered heart."[2]

One of the places I struggle most with hurry is in airports. For people with hurry sickness, an airport is like a hit of cocaine for an addict; the slow lines and waiting are like an extreme sport. Whether it's checking in luggage, going through security, boarding, putting luggage in the overhead compartment, deplaning, or strategically positioning yourself in baggage claim, a hurry junkie is always looking to shave a few seconds off the experience.

My hurried spirit also regularly reveals itself in ministry. At Saddleback we had a large patio area just outside our worship center. In a church that size, with that many services, there were always people looking for help. Sometimes it was as simple as wanting to know where to sign up for a small group or where to take their children. At times it was our leaders wanting information about an upcoming event. Other times it was a prayer request or some kind of personal crisis.

I began to notice every single conversation on the patio started out the same way: "I know you're busy, but . . ." Was I not really listening well? Was I looking past them to the next person? Was my body language restless and fidgety? I'm not sure what tipped them off, but people sure were getting the message that I was in a hurry and really didn't have time for them.

It's not easy to slow down our lives. Despite all our lamenting about how busy we are and the pace we maintain, we like exhilaration. It makes us feel important. We like pushing the envelope, and we like the adrenaline rush of a full life. Even in moments we think we'd like to get off the treadmill, we're not quite sure what we would give up. How do you slow down in a world that just keeps speeding up and offering you more?

A stuck accelerator has huge implications for my soul and my ministry. Hurry is a devious soul enemy. Incessant activity will drain us. In our rush to accomplish much and live to the fullest, we rob ourselves of some of life's richest moments.

Thomas Kelly talked about this incessant pull to try and do it all.

> We feel honestly the pull of many obligations and try to fulfill them all. And we are unhappy, uneasy, strained, oppressed and fearful we shall be shallow. . . . We have hints that there is a way of life vastly richer and deeper than all this hurried existence, a life of unhurried serenity and peace and power.[3]

What's most amazing about those words is they were written in 1941. If they were relevant then, they are even more so today.

I have come to this fundamental conviction: Following Jesus cannot be done at a sprint. You can't live life at warp speed without warping your soul.

Since this issue of "hurry" has been on my radar in recent years, I've noticed something in the life of Jesus. He never seems in a hurry.

One advantage Jesus had was that "slow" was built into the fabric of ancient life.

Think about how much slower life was in those days. When the Bible says in Mark 10:46 that they came to Jericho, this was an all day trip spent walking along the dusty road. The lack of technology and transportation forced life to be slower. The lack of cars, planes, e-mail, and smart phones made it easier to take your time. You and I live in a different world; therefore we must be even more intentional about slowing down.

What would it look like for you to "unstick" your life's accelerator?

Questions for Discussion and Reflection

1. Where does *hurry* show up in your life and ministry? What would the people who know you best say?

2. "Hurry is a devious soul enemy." In what ways is that true in your own life? In your ministry life?

3. How might your ministry change if you learned to slow down?

4. What would it look like for you to "unstick" your life's (and your ministry's) accelerator? Share one practical way you could slow down this week.

ten

FATIGUED, FRAZZLED, AND FRIED

E verywhere I go I meet people who want a simpler life, a slower pace, and a schedule with more breathing room. People are exhausted and frazzled.

For some reason, in our culture we have swallowed hook, line, and sinker the lie that busyness equals importance. I have not been exempt.

I have a love/hate relationship with my busyness. I hate being hurried and hassled by an overcrowded schedule, but I also love being in demand and love the adrenaline rush of a fast-paced life.

I have a history of taking on too much. I constantly try to figure out how to get more done, and I have a hard time sitting still. My wife tells me I don't know how to relax. I have often worn my busyness like a badge of honor. After all, if you're a committed leader for the cause of Christ, there is no time to waste.

For years I intuitively knew my obsessive busyness was violating my soul. Constant activity could prop up the external image

I wanted to project, but it couldn't prop up my soul. In honest and quiet moments, I longed to get off the treadmill and didn't know how.

I remember when I first began pastoring and got a late call or two to let me know of a crisis or of a member who had passed away. One of those calls came at 2:30 a.m. When I picked up the phone, the member said, "Pastor, I'm sorry to wake you up in the middle of the night." My knee-jerk, dysfunctional response was, "That's okay. I wasn't asleep." Actually, I was sound asleep, but my reflex reaction was to communicate, "I know it's 2:30 in the morning, but I don't sleep. I am Super Pastor, and I am always busy."

In Africa, when white men began to show up, the Swahili invented a unique, descriptive word: *mazungu*, which means "one who spins around." There are a lot of *mazungu* ministry leaders in our generation. They are a flurry of activity.

But here's the problem. Busyness will not only distract, it will infect. Your busyness will damage your soul. Over time you will develop a hurried spirit. And even when your body is still, your soul will be racing. Your busy spirit will constantly remind you of everything you need to be doing. At times you'll feel like your insides are racing.

Psalm 46:10 has only eight words and twenty-four letters, but it stands as an indictment to modern ministry: *"BE STILL, AND KNOW THAT I AM GOD."*

To look at most pastors or ministry leaders, you would think the verse said "be busy, and know that you are productive" or "work hard, and know that your ministry is successful." This verse is more about my connection *to* God than my work *for* God.

For most of my ministry, I have been great at busyness and lousy at stillness.

From the gospel of Luke, let's allow Jesus to weigh in on this topic.

It is the familiar story of two sisters, one serving and one sitting.

One is uptight; one is up close. Martha is hurrying up, and Mary is just hanging out.

Now, as far as we know, Jesus did not give any advance notice of his visit. He didn't e-mail or call ahead on his cell phone. His visit may have been a little unnerving to Mary, Martha, and Lazarus. I mean, how would you like God to drop by for an unannounced lunch? And it wasn't just Jesus; he also brought twelve hairy, dusty, grimy Galilean men.

We would be scrambling to pick up dirty clothes, tossing plates in the dishwasher, trying to figure out what refreshments could be thrown together at the last minute.

Martha is the consummate hostess. She doesn't have anything prepared, but it won't be long and she'll whip up something to eat.

Then, in the flurry of her preparations, she looks around and notices Mary isn't helping at all. In fact, Mary's *sitting*. Just sitting and listening to what Jesus has to say.

That ticks Martha off. I like Martha. Every pastor loves to have Marthas in the congregation. They get stuff done.

Martha would have loved to sit and chit-chat, but a meal must be prepared. It doesn't take long for her irritation to boil to the surface. Finally, she can't stand it anymore, and she pops off to Jesus. "It's just not right. I am in the kitchen doing everything by myself. Would you please tell Mary to come and help me?"

Jesus' response is more than a little shocking: "Martha, Martha, you are worried and upset about many things, but only one thing is needed. Mary has chosen what is better."[1]

Could it be that in our driven, overachieving busyness we have missed what's most important? Could it really be that sitting is better? It feels so unproductive.

Notice the irony. You would think the issue would be whether the God of the universe has time to sit with us, not whether we can squeeze him into our schedule.

At the peak of my own struggle with busyness, all I did was

work. Even more pathetic was that all I wanted to do was work. Any desire for hobbies, vacation, or recreation had gone dormant. Busyness was driving my life and was dragging my soul, kicking and screaming.

I can relate to Wayne Cordeiro's observation from his own journey.

> It's a gift to be able to launch an inspiring vision. But unless you manage it along the way, it can turn on you, and soon the voracious appetite of the vision consumes you.[2]

Your ministry will take all you give it. Your church will take all you are willing to give it. Ministry demands will always exceed your capacity.

I'm reminded of a great line from *Jurassic Park*. Jeff Goldblum, talking about the creation of these dinosaurs, says, "Your scientists were so preoccupied with whether or not they could, they didn't stop to think if they should."[3] Just because you can doesn't mean you should. It's a mistake to chase after every opportunity.

So, what do you do? Most of us in ministry live with a constant low-grade guilt. We know we need a better rhythm and a saner pace. We often lament our situation and talk about cutting back. But those who have slain the beast of busyness are few.

I don't have all the answers to this huge problem, but I do know you won't gradually merge into the slow lane. You have to get serious and declare war on the compulsive busyness that's controlling you.

In 1976 Peter Finch starred in *Network*. As a news broadcaster in a time of economic and social upheaval, he encouraged people to go to their windows, stick their head out, and yell, "I'm as mad as hell, and I'm not gonna take this anymore!"[4]

If we're going to turn the tide, it's going to take some leaders who get good and mad and decide they're not going to take it anymore. No one is holding a gun to our heads, forcing us to over-commit and over-schedule. As leaders, we must have the guts to start making some changes in our personal lives and church programs.

There is a simpler, less frantic way to do ministry. And, more importantly, there is a simpler, less frantic way to do life.

Questions for Discussion and Reflection

1. How would you describe the pace of your life over the past month?

2. How has busyness impacted the health of your soul? Your relationships?

3. Wayne Cordeiro said, "It's a gift to be able to launch an inspiring vision. But unless you manage it along the way, it can turn on you, and soon the voracious appetite of the vision consumes you." In what ways can vision "turn on you"?

4. From a practical perspective, what would it look like for you to do life and ministry at a reasonable pace?

eleven

IT'S NOT ALL ABOUT
THE WEEKEND

A few years ago there was a now famous conference session titled "It's About the Weekend, Stupid." It was intended to raise the value and importance of what happens in our services. Churches spend enormous resources and energies to pull off services every week. And great God moments do happen in them, so it should be important to us.

However, I think the premise is flawed. It leads you to believe that well-produced services, creative teaching, engaging music, and high-tech presentation are what make or break the church. Those can all be factors in getting more people to show up, but they are no indicator of how healthy or spiritually powerful a church is. If "it" is about making disciples, the weekend service is only one small part of the equation.

If I've learned anything about the health of churches in the last several years it's this: The weekend experience is a poor indicator of the health of a church. In fact, attendance alone is not a good gauge of effectiveness for any ministry event.

As a pastor for the last thirty years I know that we pastors tend to live and die by weekend services. If attendance is up, we feel good. If attendance is down, we wonder what's wrong. I can't begin to tell you how many times my emotions Sunday afternoon were directly connected to how many people attended that morning. Now that I've been away from the senior pastor role for the last few years, I see this issue more clearly and better understand its residual impact on the entire church.

By focusing so much on weekend services and attendance, my identity and worth got entangled with how many people showed up. My sense of personal significance and ministry impact swayed with the attendance numbers.

This was heightened by weekend attendance being the ultimate measuring stick in the world of ministry. It's often the trump card in conversations and the basis upon which people get invited to speak at national conferences and write books. We assume that because it's drawing large crowds, a church is healthy, effective, and making disciples.

Now, here's where this conversation begins to bury many pastors. They apply the same logic to their stagnant church. They assume the lack of large crowds means they're ineffective and unhealthy. They must not be doing something right; they must be a failure.

Recently, after I finished speaking at an event, I sat down next to a pastor who's been a casual acquaintance through the years. He had a somber, defeated look; you could see the discouragement on his face. He's around fifty and has been serving in the same church of about two hundred for sixteen years. He serves in a small town with a lot of problems. He faithfully preaches the gospel, and he effectively shepherds his flock.

His will never be a mega-church. At his age he's wondering if he's stuck there for the rest of his ministry. Much of his discouragement has to do with the size of his church and the fact that ministry hasn't turned out like he'd hoped. The numbers game can mess with your head and heart and end up making you feel like a loser.

We often defend our numbers obsession with statements like "there's a whole book in the Bible called Numbers" or "numbers represent people." But somehow when you hear them talked about, it doesn't always feel like it's about people. It can feel like it's more about the leader.

Too much focus on weekend attendance has one of two results, and neither is good. The pastor ends up feeling either proud or discouraged.

In 1 Corinthians 3, Paul talks about the judgment seat of Christ, where as a believer my reward will be determined. Christ's fundamental question here will be, "What did you do with what I gave you?"

> *[A man's] work will be shown for what it is, because the Day will bring it to light. It will be revealed with fire, and the fire will test the quality of each man's work.*[1]

Notice that Paul doesn't say the "quantity" of my works will be judged, but rather the "quality" of my works.

In ministry we need to recapture the word *faithful*. It is the nature of our world to be enamored with what's big. But in the church we should seek to be enamored with what's godly. By God's sovereign design and call, some people are given hard assignments where the soil is hard and the plowing is slow.

So, how do we turn the tide? How do I shift my perspective?

- It has to start with me and inside me. I have to take responsibility for and ownership of my attitude toward ministry. I have to feed my soul and make sure my identity is firmly rooted in Christ and not in my performance. I have to embrace the truth that my worth to God is not dependent on the size of my church or the number of people who attend weekend services.

- Talk more about making disciples than about attendance. I must begin to incrementally shift my church's terminology and culture away from the culture of the world. In the kingdom, size does not equal success, and growth is not synonymous with God's blessing. Our mandate is to make disciples—fully devoted, surrendered, maturing followers of Jesus. Increasingly we must shift the spotlight from the statistics of attendance to stories of life change. We must focus more on the bride's beauty and character and less on her size.

- Consider a numbers fast. I have known a couple of pastors who, in order to break their preoccupation with weekend attendance, fasted from reports about it. For a season they decided to focus on what was happening in their services rather than how many showed up.

- Bless and celebrate a pastor serving in a difficult assignment. We must do a better job of breaking down the walls of competition between churches. Many of God's choicest servants faithfully serve and preach and evangelize and shepherd in tough places. Bless them!

- Take the pressure off you and your team. It really *isn't* all about the weekend. Our pursuit of excellence (or at times perfectionism) creates a lot of stress in the team. Remind yourself and your team that your ministry is bigger and broader than those hours on Sunday. Relax. Even if this week's services don't go great, you're always just seven days away from another chance.

Questions for Discussion and Reflection

1. How does your ministry currently measure success? What gets celebrated?

2. Should your ministry adjust its view of success? If so, how?

3. Which one of the bullet points at the end of this chapter do you need to focus on? What steps can you take?

4. How much has your sense of significance been tied to your ministry's outward success?

START HERE . . .
START NOW

twelve

PIT STOPS REQUIRED

On October 25, 1999, a twin-engine Learjet taxied down the runway in Orlando on its way to Dallas. Over Gainesville, the plane should have made a left turn and headed toward Texas. But it veered off course toward South Dakota.

Repeated attempts to contact the pilots were met with a deafening silence. Five fighter planes were dispatched to go up and make visual contact.

Two F-16s finally were able to pull within fifty feet of the Learjet. The pilots reported they were unable to see inside because its windows were iced over. The plane flew on autopilot for fourteen hundred miles, over a period of four hours, and finally crashed into a grassy field at six hundred miles an hour.

All six passengers were killed, the most famous being professional golfer Payne Stewart. It was a bizarre and tragic event. Suppose for a moment you had been standing on the ground as the plane flew overhead in the clear autumn sky. It's traveling fast and straight, and as far as you know it's on course. The reality, though, is that something was desperately wrong on the inside, and it was headed for disaster.

Many ministry leaders soar through life at breakneck speed. They seem to be on course, cruising on autopilot. To the onlooker it seems they have it all together, but on the inside there is a crisis. They are on a collision course.

Solomon said, "The wisdom of the prudent is to give thought to their ways, but the folly of fools is deception."[1] One of the crying needs of ministry leaders today is to give thought to their ways and where they are headed.

Most every church or parachurch ministry I know of will take a couple of days annually to retreat and talk about plans for the future. Goals are established, initiatives are considered, resources are allocated, and course corrections are made. These leadership gatherings are crucial for the future effectiveness of the ministry.

It is just as important to do this on a personal level. As a leader I must regularly pull back from the daily grind and give thought to "my ways." My first calling is not to pay attention to the ways of the organization or the ways of the staff, but rather to my ways.

If you could plot the trajectory of your soul, your inner life, where is it headed? If your soul stays on the path it's on, where will it be ten years from now? Twenty years? After your ministry role is gone and you no longer hold an organizational position, what will you be left with? Where you end up then is largely determined by how well you manage what's going on inside you now.

A lot of ministry leaders I know are "dead people running." They're a flurry of activity, and they're working hard. But on the inside they're empty and joyless. Their trajectory has them flying toward burnout and disillusionment.

Henry Cloud's *9 Things You Simply Must Do* gives nine axioms—life lessons—that he has learned through the years. One is a principle called "Play the Movie."

Every scene in a movie is moving toward a final scene. A plot is developing. And the final scene is being shaped and determined by earlier scenes. I need to determine what kind of final scene I want and then develop a plot that gets me there.

We tend to look at life as a series of disconnected scenes. However,

> Playing the movie means never to see any individual action as a singular thing in and of itself: any one thing you do is only a scene in a larger movie.[2]

As Andy Stanley says, "Direction, not intention, determines our destination."[3] What we often fail to realize is that my life is on a path (direction) headed to a destination. What I am doing today was shaped by what I did yesterday. Who I become tomorrow will be informed by what I do today. And I am writing a scene now that will influence the final scene.

More than ever, it is imperative for leaders to take time away for thinking and reflection about where we are and where we're headed. The knee-jerk reaction for most of us is to say, "That sounds good, but I just don't have the time." If you're thinking this, I would respond that you can't afford *not* to take the time. In order to maintain my sanity and some semblance of spiritual health, I have to *make* time for personal retreat.

If you've ever watched the Indy 500, you know that no one wins the race without making pit stops. Pit stops allow the tires to be changed, adjustments to be made, and the tank to be refueled. In ministry today, we have to learn how to take personal pit stops so we can consider where we're headed and make mid-race adjustments.

Ruth Barton, in an article on personal retreat, says,

> One of the most important rhythms of a leader's life is a constant back and forth motion between times when we are engaged in the battle—giving our best energy to take the next hill—and times of retreat when we are not "on" and we do

not have to be any particular way for anyone. Time when we can be in God's presence for our own soul's sake.[4]

I recently saw an interview with Gary Haugen, who heads up the International Justice Mission. They've built an advance-and-retreat rhythm into their daily routine. Every day at eleven o'clock their staff gathers for prayer. At just the time most people would be cranking out work, they stop. They stop to pray for the enormous needs facing IJM worldwide. But they also stop to pray as a reminder that they can't do this work without God's power.

Another intriguing part of their rhythm is their eight-thirty stillness. The staff day begins at eight-thirty, but the doors don't open until nine. Haugen says, "The first half hour of every day at IJM everyone is paid to sit and do nothing. That is, to sit still and to prepare spiritually for the day with thirty minutes of solitude and reflection. The first half hour of every day is set aside for us to personally be present with God, consider the day, and prepare spiritually." They begin with daily retreat so they can be spiritually prepared to advance.

Leaders who stay spiritually healthy long term are those who learn this sacred rhythm of advance and retreat. There *are* times when we're focused on the mission and taking the next hill for Christ's kingdom. But you can't stay on the front lines forever. You have to rest and regroup. In fact, the more fierce and intense the battle, the more often you have to retreat.

For me, times of retreat have had two powerful benefits.

1. *Replenishing my soul.* When I'm on retreat, something happens inside me that's hard to explain. When I first started practicing this, being alone and being quiet was not enjoyable. Even though my body was on retreat, my mind was full throttle. All I could think about was what I needed to do. But over time I have learned to slow my spirit, and I now realize the world can get along just fine without me for a little while. I am learning

to "be" with my heavenly Father, and my soul is replenished in the process.

2. *Recalibrating my perspective.* As I ponder and pray, God regularly shifts my outlook by reminding me of what is really important. He regularly convicts me of getting so worked up over things that just aren't that important. On retreat I have removed most of the white noise from my world, and I can be quiet enough to hear God's voice.

So, how about it? Schedule a twenty-four-hour personal retreat. I promise, it won't kill you, the world will manage without you, and you will be healthier for it.

Questions for Discussion and Reflection

1. If your soul (inner life) stays on the path it's on, what will be the result ten years from now? Where will you be?

2. How have you done at taking time to pull back from daily routine and give thought to your ways?

3. How well has your ministry or church learned the sacred rhythm of advance and retreat? What steps could you take to better embrace such a rhythm?

4. If you were to take a personal retreat, what would you do on the retreat? What would you not do?

WHAT KIND OF OLD PERSON DO I WANT TO BE?

W hat kind of old person do you want to be? It's a question you never think about in your twenties, rarely in your thirties, and only occasionally in your forties. But at least in my case hitting the big five-zero caused me to ponder this question with great frequency.

Turning fifty flipped an inner switch; I found myself asking a lot more questions. Not about next year's vacation or the kind of car we might purchase or whether to change from ground beef to ground turkey. I found myself asking more *life* questions, legacy questions.

I became more self-reflective and introspective than ever before. I developed a growing awareness that the clock was ticking, and it was like I could hear the sweep of the second hand as it clicked off moments I would never recapture. I have reached that stage of life where more ministry road is in the rearview mirror than in the windshield.

It was during this new season of self-reflection that I picked up Gordon MacDonald's *The Life God Blesses*. A seasoned ministry veteran with a lot of life insight, he asked the question, "What kind of old man do you want to be?" He'd been reading the story of Caleb, who at eighty-five was described as following the Lord God of Israel "wholeheartedly."[1]

MacDonald started looking around for other older men who were at their very best in their twilight years. "One thing quickly became clear. I have known a lot of old men, but my list of 'emulatable' old men was alarmingly short."

This was true for a variety of reasons. Some had drifted into self-centeredness, while others had become impatient and cynical toward the next generation. Some had let the later years sour them into becoming grumpy and critical. Many simply lived in the past and were no longer leaning forward into the future. "When the list was finished, it included just a few names. In fact, I could count the names on the fingers of one hand."[2]

Securing a spot on MacDonald's list of "emulatable" old men had virtually nothing to do with achievement or success as we often define it. It had more to do with character and attitude and "being."

Having served in ministry more than three decades, I find myself less enamored with accomplishment and the bravado that often accompanies it. I am more drawn to men and women who live well than to those who live big. But those who've been in ministry a long time and are living well aren't that easy to find. Why aren't there more whose twilight years are their highlight years?

I think Henri Nouwen gives us a clue.

> I began to experience a deep inner threat. As I entered into my fifties and was able to realize the unlikelihood of doubling my years, I came face to face with the simple question, "Did becoming older bring me closer to Jesus?" After twenty-five years of priesthood, I found myself praying poorly, living somewhat isolated from other people, and very much

preoccupied with burning issues. Everyone was saying that I was doing really well, but something inside was telling me that my success was putting my own soul in danger.[3]

I'm intrigued by that statement: "my success was putting my own soul in danger." I've thought a lot about those words. When we have accomplished a measure of success, we can begin to coast. Pastors write thousands of sermons, lead thousands of meetings, and prepare thousands of budgets (or at least it seems like it). Twenty or twenty-five years of pushing and striving and leading take their toll. We can feel drained, fatigued, and even jaded. The thought of one more vision message or capital campaign just doesn't crank up the adrenaline like it once did.

At this point in life we're very capable of leading out of our experience and knowledge rather than the deep well of a healthy soul. On the outside we have the answers, but on the inside we have questions. To further complicate matters, our physical stamina begins to diminish.

Don't get me wrong. I'm not saying passion for ministry goes away. I am saying it feels different than when you first started. As a twenty-five-year veteran, you face a whole new set of challenges. The triple-A of adrenaline, ambition, and achievement aren't enough to sustain you anymore.

Here's the irony. At just the time most people look at you as the picture of success, you are aware of some desperately broken places in your life. Like Nouwen, we have to admit that decades of ministry haven't necessarily made us more like Jesus. Our sermons are better, our leadership is better, our staff management is better, our planning is better, but our intimacy with Jesus? Not so much.

We have a gut-wrenching choice to make. We can put our ministry on autopilot and move into image-management mode. Or we can do the hard work of reinventing ourselves, of reworking the last chapters of life. If you have been drinking at the well of ambition and success and drivenness . . . that well will run dry. It's time to drill a new well that will sustain you as you get older.

For many of us in ministry, our challenge is quite different. It's not success that threatens our soul but the perceived *lack* of success that now becomes the threat to us as we age. Ministry hasn't turned out like we thought it would. We've done the best we could, but more often than we want to admit, ministry has been more babysitting than leading, more mundane than miraculous, more life-taking than life-giving.

Some days we want out. We daydream about what it's like on the outside. We fantasize about a prison break from the constraints of ministry. We wonder what it would be like to have a "normal" life. We ponder how it would feel to have weekends off. We dream of not being constantly scrutinized.

If ministry hasn't turned out like you expected, I want to ask you the same question. What kind of old man or woman do you want to be? I'm not asking what kind of ministry you want to have. I'm asking about you, as a person, as a Christ follower. You can't undo the past, and you can't control all of your circumstances, but you can plot a different trajectory for your future.

Questions for Discussion and Reflection

1. Who is an older person you would like to emulate? What about them makes you want to be like them?

2. As you think of what kind of old person you want to be, what top three qualities would you like to be true of you in your twilight years?

3. Is there any place in your life or ministry where you've begun to coast? Explain.

4. What does "finishing well" mean to you? What adjustments will you need to make to finish well?

fourteen

IT'S ALL ABOUT
THE GROOM

When my daughter got married, I performed the ceremony, and people have often asked what that was like. I usually say, "It was emotionally and financially devastating." Don't get me wrong, it was one of the highlights of my life and one I will always treasure deeply. There was no question my daughter (as she should have been) was the center of attention. I have the photos and bills to prove it.

In contemporary Western culture, the bride is the centerpiece of every wedding ceremony. She wears the long flowing dress, she enters to a "bridal march," she parades down the center aisle with the pomp and circumstance reserved for kings, and people stand as she enters. It's clearly all about the bride.

The lowly groom, on the other hand, is an afterthought. He's filler, the warm-up act for the main attraction. Unlike the bride, he usually enters from a side door. He wears a tux that some other groom will be wearing next weekend. And, for him, there is no grand march—he often enters to what strikingly resembles elevator music.

The way we do weddings today is quite different from the weddings of the Bible, especially the relationship between Christ and his bride, the church.

The book of Revelation describes the mother of all wedding scenes. But here it is the groom who gets all the attention.

> *Let us rejoice and be glad and give him glory! For the wedding of the Lamb has come, and his bride has made herself ready.*[1]

It is the wedding of the Lamb, not the wedding of the bride.

A couple of verses later, the apostle John writes, *Blessed are those who are invited to the wedding supper of the Lamb!*[2] The spotlight is fixed firmly on the groom, Jesus.

When John the Baptist settles an argument about his position in relationship to Jesus, he uses wedding imagery to set the record straight. In no uncertain terms, he declares he is simply a friend of the groom, that Jesus is the center of attention.

But he also makes an interesting statement about the bride.

> *The bride belongs to the bridegroom. The friend who attends the bridegroom waits and listens for him, and is full of joy when he hears the bridegroom's voice. That joy is mine, and it is now complete.*[3]

The bride belongs to the groom. That's not only a statement about ancient marriage ritual, it's also a great picture of the relationship between the church and Jesus.

This has huge implications for how we view the church in our generation and how we view our roles as leaders in it.

In the last thirty years within the church world, there has been a subtle shifting of the spotlight. Inadvertently, in many places, it has become all about the bride (the church) rather than the groom (Jesus). But, as John reminds us, the bride belongs to the bridegroom. Or to say it another way, the bride exists for the groom.

As a pastor, then, my job is to watch after the bride on behalf of the groom. I am like a spiritual wedding coordinator. The coordinator's job is to assist and serve the bride and groom, behind the scenes, in making their wedding day a meaningful event.

No wedding coordinator worth their salt would ever steal the spotlight from the bride and groom. Jesus said, "Father, I want these whom you've given me to be with me, so they can see my glory. You gave me the glory because you loved me even before the world began!"[4]

There should never be anything blocking the bride's view of the Groom's glory. My constant challenge as a leader in the church is to get myself out of the way so that the bride will be awestruck by the incomparable majesty of her Groom.

One of the indicators of spiritual disease in a church leader is a possessive spirit about the bride. You can hear it in their words, you can feel it in their attitude, and you can read it in their decisions. The church is "theirs."

It's helpful for me to remind myself regularly that the church is not "mine." I am a steward . . . Yes! I am a shepherd . . . Yes! I am a leader . . . Yes! But, I am not the owner, CEO, title-holder, or groom of the church.

The bride belongs to the bridegroom. Thus, the church is not my personal trophy or sandbox or project. I hold it as a sacred trust to steward on behalf of the groom, who's asked me to look after his bride until he comes for her.

I remember having a conversation with a guy who'd entered ministry after a very successful business career. We were talking about his pastor being exempt from some church policies, and at that point this man's only frame of reference was the world of big business. "I have no problem," he said, "with the pastor playing by different rules. After all, he is the founder and owner of the company."

I was taken aback by his perspective and came back strongly: "Your pastor is not the founder or owner of the church. Jesus is the founder, and he owns the church by virtue of the fact he purchased it with his blood. Your church is not your pastor's personal business venture. He is an undershepherd called to care for the sheep on behalf of the owner."

In a healthy church Jesus is the most famous person. He gets the most airtime, he is the most talked about, and he is clearly center stage. He is seen as the head of the church, and the leadership does their best to spread his fame.

Is your place in ministry blocking the spotlight from hitting squarely on Jesus? When the leader's role or importance is overemphasized, a subtle shift can take place in our minds and spirits. We can start to play the role of owner rather than steward.

When things get really unhealthy, we can step in front of the groom and put the spotlight on us. One of the definitions of presumption is "behavior that is inconsiderate, disrespectful, or overconfident." It is the height of presumption when the very people God has called to shine the spotlight on the bride and groom shine it on themselves.

Like John Piper says, "Christ does not exist to make much of us. We exist in order to enjoy making much of Him."[5]

Questions for Discussion and Reflection

1. How well has your ministry or church done at keeping Jesus front and center? What has at times gotten in the way?

2. How does seeing your role as wedding coordinator impact how you do ministry?

3. What does it mean for you to hold your ministry as a sacred trust?

4. What can you do to keep from being too possessive and taking too much ownership of your ministry?

fifteen

THE CALL NO ONE
WANTS TO GET

K evin Skinner was obscure—absolutely anonymous—until
he won the million dollars. An unemployed chicken catcher
who loved to write songs, he won the top prize on *America's Got
Talent*.

It's the stuff dreams are made of. We love it when the underdog
becomes top dog. We love it when somebody small makes it big.
Maybe it's because we picture ourselves standing on the stage and
performing in front of the cheering crowds.

I'd be lying if I told you I haven't had those pictures run through
my mind. The truth is, being known, admired, and respected makes
us feel important. But what if God's plan isn't to give me a Kevin
Skinner moment? What if my calling is to relative obscurity?

Obscurity can be a bitter pill to swallow. We in ministry like
to quote passages like the one in Acts 17 that says the early church
turned the world upside down.[1] We love to talk about great people
of faith who changed their world. Hebrews 11 talks about such
people. These great men and women of faith conquered kingdoms,

shut the mouths of lions, quenched the fury of the flames, became powerful in battle, routed foreign armies, and even raised the dead to life.

It would be great if the chapter ended there, leaving us inspired by the exponential potential of faith. But there's a ninety-degree turn in the middle of verse 35, a subtle transition in the word "others."

Their names are not listed. They will remain historically anonymous. These "others" were still great men and women of faith. In fact, "the world was not worthy of them."[2] But unlike those who experienced miracles and victory, these "others" were tortured, flogged, imprisoned, stoned, and put to death by the sword. They were destitute, often homeless, and they lived in obscurity.

Interestingly, "These were all commended for their faith, yet none of them received what had been promised."[3] None of them received what had been promised. *Not yet.* Not in this world. Not all of God's promises had been fulfilled in this life.

But this life is not all there is. For them, their faith hadn't delivered them from death; their faith caused their death. Their faith didn't bring fame; it brought danger. And following Jesus did not bring notoriety; it brought obscurity.

One of the spiritual health questions every ministry leader must answer is, "Am I willing to serve in obscurity?"

The first church I pastored was small, rural, and obscure. I came there fresh out of seminary. I was naïve, optimistic, full of ambition. After five years, though, my grandiose visions had degenerated into the hard work of pastoring. I wanted out.

During those days I remember flying to Dallas to interview with a church about a possible position. The interview took place at a hotel, and afterward I walked into the lobby and called my wife. I told her, "If I were them, I would not hire me. I am not what they are looking for." Sure enough, the following Tuesday I received the call that I knew was coming. Even so, it was devastating. I vividly remember sitting at my desk and weeping like a baby. I didn't want to be anonymous. I wanted to be sought out, not left out. Obscurity was not part of my plan.

I eventually did move to another church. I wish I could tell you I had learned to be fully content where I was and then God moved me. That wouldn't be true. But in those days God began a work that continues to this day.

Looking back, I see that obscurity allowed me to wrestle with my identity and significance.

In her insightful book *Anonymous*, Alicia Britt Chole says, "From God's perspective, anonymous seasons are sacred spaces.... Unapplauded, but not unproductive: hidden years are the surprising birthplace of true spiritual greatness."[4] This was certainly true of Jesus. We tend to forget that the stories about him reflect a very short time period. The overwhelming majority of his life was spent in total obscurity. Only for a short season was he in the public eye.

> Jesus was born in Bethlehem in a smelly animal pen (followed by hidden days). He was circumcised in the temple on his eighth day (followed by hidden months). Before turning two, Jesus received a visit from Eastern wise men (followed by hidden years). At the age of twelve he teaches in the temple (followed by almost two entirely hidden decades).[5]

Jesus never ran toward the spotlight. He never focused on drawing a large crowd or marketing his brand. He knew that unseen does not equal unimportant. It's been a long time coming, but I am learning to embrace this truth.

Here is something else I'm learning. Even if you've had a "Kevin Skinner" moment where the spotlight has been on you, it doesn't last long. The spotlight is fickle. It will always turn toward the next rising star. Even if you're in the spotlight today, obscurity is coming again. It's inevitable.

When the spotlight is gone, what you have left is the relationship. That's why paying attention to your soul is so important.

Someday the trappings of ministry will fade away, and all you'll have will be Jesus. Will that be enough?

Yesterday I was on a flight with a quite elderly lady. When she got out into baggage claim, her husband was sitting on a bench waiting for her. When he saw her, he lit up like a Christmas tree. With cane in hand he moved toward her and kissed her like a newlywed. It was awesome.

I don't know what kind of life this couple has shared. They might have had a successful business. They could have made a lot of money. They might have been famous for all I know.

But now they're in their twilight years. Their looks have faded. Their physical strength is diminished. There was no fanfare upon her return. No limo, no media, no spotlight. There was just one person to greet her, but it was the one person with whom she'd shared her life. They have each other, and that's enough.

Obscurity didn't matter. The relationship did.

Someday the trappings of ministry will fade away. We'll move out of the office. We won't have a business card or a title. The spotlight will turn to someone else. But if we've been sharing our life with Jesus, obscurity won't matter. The relationship will.

If you're in a time of obscurity now, God has not forgotten you. Even though you might be hidden from the world, you are not hidden from him. Allow this anonymous season to deepen rather than discourage you. Don't chase after the spotlight; chase after the relationship.

This prayer names what's often in my heart and helps me embrace my obscurity.

> Today I still long so much for honour, I am so pleased with myself, so rooted in my nature. I am pleased when others ask for my opinion, when I am made to feel I am needed, when people know that I am clever, talented and popular. I am glad when I am friends with everyone, when I can share what is in my heart, when I can shine.

But Lord Jesus, you were a servant of all. Today I surrender all desire to be great; I renounce all pleasure I take in being important.[6]

Questions for Discussion and Reflection

1. Who is someone you admire for faithfulness to God in obscurity? Describe their faith.

2. Was there a time when you felt forgotten by God? What was that time like?

3. How are you preparing now for the time when all you'll have will be Jesus?

4. In what ways has God shaped you during times of obscurity?

sixteen

SIMPLICITY IS NOT SIMPLE

I love going into model homes. But not for the reason you might think. I like them because they're a clutter-free zone. No trash, no piles, no stacks. The kitchen counters aren't littered with small appliances and week-old bananas. For neat freaks, model homes are utopia.

The problem with a model home is that it's an illusion. Families create messes. Model homes aren't real life. That's the way I often feel about the topic of simplicity. The image of an uncluttered, ordered life sounds great, but it just doesn't seem like real life.

Let's face it. Life—and ministry—feels anything but simple these days.

Maybe you can resonate with the words of Charles Wagner: "Amid the confused restlessness of modern life, our wearied minds dream of simplicity."[1] It is mind-boggling that he wrote those words in Paris in 1895, before the invention of the car, the airplane, the TV, the computer, or the internet.

The world is not going to slow down. Technology is not going away; 24/7 access to everything is here to stay. Life and ministry are more complex and challenging than ever.

Yet inside me is a quiet longing for something simpler.

For most of my life, simplicity has felt elusive. In fact, it's rarely been on my radar. If I'm honest, I thought simplicity and margin were for navel-gazers and underachievers. There was a badge of honor in taking on too much, living too fast, and working unreasonable hours.

When I was exhausted and stressed, I'd often deceive myself with, "It'll get better. This is only for a season." But it didn't get better. And when one season of ministry was finished, it was simply replaced with a new season of demands and pressures.

At least for me, the first step toward simplicity was taking full responsibility. I had to own my stuff and admit that when it comes to simplicity I am my own worst enemy. Most of the complexity and clutter was my own doing—saying yes to too many requests, not having healthy boundaries, not knowing my limits, and always trying to please everyone contributed to a cluttered life.

I was not the victim, I was the perpetrator. No elder board or deacon group or staff member or spouse or friend was going to simplify my life for me.

I also have to realize I will never drift toward simplicity. The drift is always toward complexity and clutter. Take your garage, for example. If you neglect it, it will naturally drift toward disorder.

Pursuing simplicity is like trying to keep barnacles off a ship. These unseen, unwanted passengers clandestinely attach themselves to the hull and cause significant drag. Did you know barnacles cost the U.S. Navy about a billion dollars a year in extra fuel and maintenance?

We must be proactive and preemptive in guarding our lives from complexity.

So, how do you do this, practically? You get crystal clear about your values and priorities.

Mindy Caliguire writes, "Simplicity means taking action to align one's exterior world with one's interior values and commitment to God."[2] When my values get clear, decisions get simple. Not easy, but simple. Simplicity is not necessarily about doing less. It's about using your priorities to filter opportunities and options.

One of my biggest challenges is learning to say no. I love ministry, and I love serving churches. So when opportunities come along, my default response is yes. I think to myself, *I really don't have the bandwidth for this, but I'll figure out a way to get it done.* This mindset has added complexity to my life and stress to my marriage.

Because this is such an ongoing struggle for me, it's important for me to step back regularly and evaluate my activity in light of my priorities. Just this week I had two men I respect speak into my life about this issue. Their observation was that my focus was diffused and fragmented, and they challenged me to simplify. They were right, and their candid feedback was a gift. I am learning that a diffused life is a confused life.

As the German artist Hans Hofmann eloquently said, "The ability to simplify means to eliminate the unnecessary so that the necessary may speak." That's exactly what my friends were telling me to do. By removing those things that really aren't a priority in my life, I will create space for the "necessary" to speak. I must trim the excess so there is room for the essential.

- *Own your life.* Take responsibility, and don't play the victim card. The problem is internal, not environmental.
- *Get alone and determine your values and priorities.* Write them down and regularly review them.
- *Make the hard decisions.* The hardest part is having the courage to carry out the necessary decisions that will help you simplify.
- *Perform regular maintenance.* Practice the discipline of planned neglect.

I've devised a formula that helps me in my pursuit of simplicity: Clarity + Courage + Calendar = Simplicity.

First, I must get clarity around what's really important in my life. Because of our drift toward clutter and complexity, this must be revisited on a regular basis.

But it's not enough to simply have clarity. I must also have the courage to execute based on clarity. I can have clarity around my priorities, but without the courage to make the necessary changes, I will not move toward simplicity. Finally, the courage to execute gets very practical when I calendarize my priorities.

Five Guys, the famous East Coast hamburger chain, understands simplicity. On their website is the question, "Does Five Guys plan to add any menu items (i.e., milkshakes, chili, etc.)?"

Their answer: "Five Guys does not currently have plans to add any items to our menu. We follow the philosophy of focusing on a few items, and serving them to the best of our ability. If we were to add to our menu, then you can guarantee that we would only do so if we could serve the highest quality product possible. For example, there are a lot of great milkshakes out there, and at this point we think that others are doing it better than we could!"[3]

They are clear about who they are and clear about who they aren't. They've resisted chasing after every opportunity. The result is focus, simplicity, and a really great burger.

Questions for Discussion and Reflection

1. Does your life feel more like a model home or a cluttered garage? Explain.

2. What are the barnacles that work against simplicity in your life? In your ministry?

3. What would simplicity look like for you? Share a couple of your nonnegotiable priorities/values.

4. What is the "unnecessary" that you need to eliminate so that the "necessary" can speak in your life?

seventeen

FEEL THE RHYTHM

The other day I was Skyping with a pastor from Argentina. I asked him what I should know about the pastors who would be attending our upcoming conference. He said, "They are weary and overscheduled with too many meetings and church activities."

Ministry fatigue is not isolated to the suburban American mega-church. Fatigue is a constant theme I hear regardless of the size of town or the size of church. There are many Christian leaders who are living AWOL (A Worn-Out Life). I talk with a lot of pastors, and I can see it in their eyes, hear it in their voices, and read it in their body language.

If we do slow down we have this low-grade nagging guilt that we aren't being "productive." We can't relax. We can't sit still. We can't stop checking Twitter. We can't *stop*. It's ironic that those who should model and lead others to a healthy rhythm of life are themselves in bondage to busyness.

The grass always looks greener and more restful in somebody else's ministry. "If I had a smaller church, I would have a lot less hassle . . . and life would be a lot easier." "If I had that much staff and budget, I wouldn't have to do everything myself . . . and life would be a lot easier."

While we regularly lament the pace and pressure of ministry, we aren't quite sure how to stop the treadmill. We cope the best we can but we sure wish it could be different. The fatigue we feel on the surface often masks a deep longing underneath. It's not only a longing for a different kind of ministry but also for a different kind of life. A life that is both sane and satisfying . . . a life that works.

But life doesn't work when we are constantly busy. Over time our spiritual and emotional reserves get depleted. When we are depleted, we lose our way.

A poem Ruth Barton shares reveals how loss of rhythm causes us to lose our way.

> Holy One,
> There is something I wanted to tell you
> But there have been errands to run, bills to pay,
>   arrangements to make, meetings to attend, friends to
>   entertain, washing to do . . .
> And I forget what it is I wanted to say to you, and
>   mostly I forget what I'm about, or why.[1]

I have rewritten this prayer as follows to reflect those of us who lead in ministry:

> Holy One,
> There is something I wanted to tell you
> But there have been events to plan, e-mails to return,
>   ministry goals to submit, talks to prepare, conflicts
>   to resolve, church members to counsel . . .
> And I forget what it is I wanted to say to you, and
>   mostly I forget what I'm about . . . or why.

This topic is not just theoretical for me. I have suffered the self-inflicted wounds of an insane pace. I remember a fellow pastor saying to me one day, "Saddleback is like Las Vegas. It never shuts down. We're open 24/7."

His observation was spot on. If you know anything about casinos, you know that historically they were built without any windows. The idea is you don't want the people gambling to have a sense of time. You don't want them to distinguish daylight from dark. In a casino there is no sense of rhythm. And some of us have casino-like ministries.

The key to unlocking a sane pace of life is found in that word "rhythm."

We do not live in a casino. We live in a universe that flows with rhythm. The tide comes in, the tide goes out. The sun comes up, the sun goes down. The seasons come, the seasons go. The kids grow up, the kids move out (we hope). This idea of rhythm is central to God instituting the Sabbath.

After God created the world, the Bible says he Sabbathed (rested). He did so not because he was worn out from creation, but to model for us a rhythm of work and rest.

Noah benShea writes, "It's the space between the notes that makes the music."[2] The same is true of life. We must have space between the notes (rhythm) to make life work as God designed it.

Jesus regularly took time to live in the spaces between the notes. He often withdrew from the demands of life to be alone and to be with his Father. He also helped the disciples embrace the idea of rhythm.

> Come away to a deserted place all by yourselves and rest for a while.[3]

The last few years I've been working more intentionally to create space between the notes. I am learning the rhythms of Sabbath, personal retreat, and quiet reflection. I certainly haven't mastered the art of rhythm, but my life is less frantic and fatigued.

Productivity and achieving don't consume me like they used

to. My internal RPMs aren't red-lining like they used to. It feels good. It feels more sustainable.

I want to challenge you to really stare this issue in the face. If you're like me, it's probably taking more of a toll than you know. Your good intention must become a decision, a decision to create space between the notes of busyness. Sit down and have heart to heart conversations with your spouse, your staff, your kids, and your dog about the changes you're going to make.

The Jews have a Sabbath tradition, called the Havdalah, that reflects the benefit of living a life of rhythm. The Havdalah takes place at the conclusion of Sabbath. It's customary to spill some of the Sabbath wine into a saucer, and then to extinguish the candle by dipping it into the wine. Spilling wine into the saucer was to symbolize the Sabbath's influence spilling over into the rest of the week.

If you can begin to live a life of rhythm, the benefits will spill over into every area of your life. If you can start to create some spaces between the notes, you will discover that the noise of your life will actually turn into music.

Questions for Discussion and Reflection

1. When did you have the best sense of healthy rhythm in your life?

2. How would you describe the rhythm of your life over the last three months?

3. Describe what a life of rhythm would look like for you.

4. When you read the poem "Holy One," what do you think and feel?

iPHONES AND YOUR SOUL

I have a love/hate relationship with technology. Even though I'm not very tech savvy, I'm a sucker for a new gadget. I like being organized and staying on top of my world. I like having instant and round-the-clock access to the web and e-mail and calendar and bank accounts. Technology helps me be more productive and efficient.

The good news for gadget junkies is there's an endless stream of new and improved technologies to feed our addiction. Just consider the development of applications. Before the end of 2010 there were over 250,000 apps for the iPhone.

I recently was in a meeting with a group of pastors where everyone brought a laptop. One of the first questions was, "What's the password for the wireless router?" Going a couple of hours without being connected was unthinkable and unacceptable.

At one point I noticed something disturbing; remember, this was a live meeting with real people discussing important issues about the church. I realized I was multi-tasking. I had several screens open. I was answering time-sensitive e-mails. I checked some possible flights for an upcoming trip.

I also was carrying on two different chat conversations. One was with another guy in the same meeting. (By chatting we could give commentary without anyone else knowing what we were saying.) As if that weren't enough, I was regularly checking my phone for text messages. And I was engaged in the live discussion. I am a sick person!

But I suspect you can probably relate to my dysfunction. Technology is dominating our world, and it's not going away.

How do we leverage technology's benefits without letting it create dysfunction in our lives and teams? How do we utilize technology so that it's helpful and not harmful?

The starting place, I believe, is to recognize its limitations and the possible side effects of too much technology.

Constant connection creates internal as well as external noise. No wonder we struggle with spiritual practices like Sabbath and solitude and prayer and meditation. Even when we turn off the gadgets, we can't seem to turn off the noise inside. We're restless, fidgety, and edgy.

If you don't believe me, just try being quiet for five minutes. Turn off everything and sit quietly. Seriously, try it. If you're like me, this is no easy assignment. My mind quickly races to all that is going on in my world. Five minutes seems like five hours.

> There was a time when silence was normal and a lot of racket disturbed us. But today, noise is the normal fare, and silence, strange as it may seem, has become the real disturbance.[1]

Not only does technology generate a lot of internal white noise, it hinders our ability to focus on people. It seems to me many of us have developed a kind of social ADD. We can't stay engaged in a conversation or an experience because we're constantly checking, monitoring, tweeting, or texting. Even though it's unintentional, we're devaluing people and cheapening relationships.

Often technology can work against relationships rather than for them. Twitter and texting and Facebook can keep me connected, but there are limitations to what can be delivered virtually. I am not able to hold the person's hand or put an arm around their shoulder. I can't communicate care and interest through eye contact. I can't hear his or her voice.

The ministry of presence is not fully possible in a virtual relationship. Sometimes the most powerful gift you can give a friend is just sitting with them, *being* there when they go through a problem.

So, with technology's limitations and potential risks, what are some practical steps we can take to cultivate health?

- *Unplug.* Literally and figuratively. Consider giving your phone and e-mail a weekly Sabbath. What would it be like if you unplugged for twenty-four hours and focused more on your visible relationships than your virtual relationships? One pastor I know tells his staff he's "going dark" when he plans to unplug for family time. If this is an area you struggle with, have a discussion with your spouse or a good friend. Ask: "How does technology sometimes get in the way of our relationship?" Then make some decisions and develop a game plan that will help you use but not abuse technology. Maybe you need to commit to not being on e-mail after you get home from work. Maybe you should commit to turn off your phone during dinner. Maybe no texting during sex. I just thought I'd throw that in to see if you were still paying attention.

- *Engage.* When you engage in conversation, listen! Make good eye contact. Don't look past people. Don't send signals through your body language that you're in a hurry. Practice being fully present. Communicate care and value by giving your full and undivided attention. While technology has its place, there is no substitute for full, personal, physical, focused—undivided—attention.

- *Treat others like you would want to be treated.* That means you aren't constantly glancing at your phone looking for the next text message. That means you don't send an e-mail when you need to have a personal conversation. That means being very discerning about answering a phone call when you're meeting with someone.

I am convinced that if Jesus were walking our planet today, he would leverage technology for the building up of the kingdom. But I'm just as convinced he would manage it well so that in building up the kingdom he didn't tear down his own soul.

Questions for Discussion and Reflection

1. How has technology helped you personally and in ministry?

2. How can technology be disruptive and detrimental to your soul?

3. How can the use of technology adversely impact your relationships?

4. What are some practical steps you can take to combat the dangers of technology to your soul?

nineteen

70% OF PASTORS DON'T HAVE ONE

Imagine a day in your future. You are now seventy or seventy-five, and the pace of life has slowed. You get up early in the morning and sit in your favorite chair with a cup of coffee. The house is still and silent. No one is there but you and God and your thoughts.

On this morning, instead of thinking about the day's activities, you begin to reflect upon the past. It's like you've popped in a DVD of your life. You see family vacations, times with your spouse, holidays spent with relatives. You have memories of ministry, both rewarding and painful. It hasn't always been easy, and not everything turned out like you hoped, but it's been a good life.

Today one thought especially encourages you and brings a smile to your face. You are grateful to God that you took time to develop a handful of deep friendships. You realize that on life's balance sheet, possessing cars, houses, and toys doesn't add up to much. But a real friendship is of high value. It's the stuff life is made of.

The truth is those of us in ministry often don't do the friendship thing very well. One survey among pastors found that 70 percent do not have a close friend, confidant, or mentor. Henri Nouwen wrote, "Most Christian leadership is exercised by people who do not know how to develop healthy, intimate relationships."[1] What an indictment.

I grew up around church and Christians, so I've always had a lot of acquaintances. My relational circle was wide but not very deep. Looking back, there were at least three factors that made deep friendship elusive.

First, my church didn't talk much about the value of community and relationship. We talked a lot about salvation and knowing the Bible and pure living. But even the challenges of pure living were mostly directed toward people "out there" in the world. It never felt like anybody inside the church had a messy life. As a result, there was a subtle pressure to project an image that you had it all together. Because of that subtle pressure you wouldn't let people get too close, which meant your friendships were usually shallow.

The second factor had to do with my personality and wiring. By nature, I am calculated and cautious when it comes to relationships. I don't let my guard down easily. Opening up and being completely transparent does not come easy for me.

The third factor that's made deep friendship hard has been "ministry." Somewhere along the way in my training, I got it in my head that as a pastor you can't (and shouldn't) have close friends in your church. You don't want to be accused of partiality by hanging out with some members more than others. And, besides, you don't want to let people peer too closely into your life and family. They might discover you *don't* have it all together.

So, for the first fifteen years of ministry I learned how to pastor and live the Christian life by keeping everyone at a safe emotional distance. I lived in denial of any deep relational needs I had. I was quite content to skim relationally and focus on building the church. Then I hit my mid-thirties.

Longings I had suppressed began to come to the surface. There was something missing, and I began to feel it. I began to have thoughts like, *God made me a man before he made me a pastor. And, as a man he made me to live in community.* I got to where I just didn't care what other people thought. I knew I had to go deeper in a few relationships, no matter how it was perceived.

Joseph Myers' *The Search to Belong* has been very helpful in my thinking about relationships, about which he talks of four categories: Public, Social, Personal, and Intimate.[2] It's important to have people in each category, and the number in each category descends from Public to Intimate. As a pastor, I'd become quite skilled at Public and Social relationships. And I was able to manage at the Personal level. But there was no friend that would have fit the Intimate category. There was no one who fully knew me, the naked truth about me.

During this season God brought into my life a pastor friend with whom I connected easily. As trust began to develop, we both decided to pursue the friendship. I learned in this process that you never drift into deep friendship.

One of the most famous friendships in Scripture is that of David and Jonathan. At one point, Jonathan does something that feels awkward and uncomfortable for most men: "*Jonathan made a special vow to be David's friend,* and he sealed the pact by giving him his robe, tunic, sword, bow, and belt."[3] He made a "special vow." He declared his commitment to pursue the friendship. We just don't do that today. For most people I know in ministry and certainly for most men, this seems way too touchy-feely.

Nevertheless, again, if I'm going to be spiritually healthy, I'm going to need an intimate friend or two who fully know me, friends who aren't impressed with me and who aren't afraid to tell me the truth. I need a handful of people who know the junk about me, who know where I struggle, who know the skeletons in my closet, and who love and accept me anyway.

This kind of friendship doesn't happen by accident. If you've got someone in your life you want to go deeper with, do what Jonathan did. Declare it! Life is too short and there is too much at stake for you to avoid this level of friendship.

Someone has said friendship is like a watermelon. The outside is hard, tough, and difficult to penetrate. The outside shell is great for protecting, but terrible for digesting. The inside is softer and more vulnerable, yet that's where the fruit is.

In *A Million Miles in a Thousand Years*, Donald Miller tells the story of Jim and Janice, who was diagnosed with cancer and didn't live long after her diagnosis. After her funeral, a lot of family friends gathered and shared stories and memories of times with her. "I wondered," Miller writes, "how much it costs to be rich in friends and how many years and stories and scenes it takes to make a rich life happen. You can't build an end scene as beautiful as this by sitting on the couch."[4]

No you can't. So, start now. Build a rich life by developing a few deep friendships.

Questions for Discussion and Reflection

1. Describe your best friend growing up. What made that relationship special?

2. Why is it hard sometimes for people in ministry to develop healthy, intimate friendships?

3. What is the biggest barrier to your going deeper with a few friends?

4. When you think of being "fully known" by a friend, what's your honest response?

twenty

IDENTITY THEFT

There's a huge difference between being a son/daughter and being an employee. A company has a transactional relationship with the employee. You produce . . . you're in. You don't produce . . . you're out. Your compensation is connected to your contribution.

But it's different being a son or daughter. You are family. Your place is not dependent on your performance. As a son, my value is intrinsic, not transactional.

For many years I did ministry as an employee rather than as a son. My value and acceptance were dependent on how well I performed. I'm not quite sure where I picked up this script, but it definitely guided my approach to ministry.

The result was the blurring of the line between my identity and my ministry. When identity gets wrapped up in ministry, you put more weight than you should in praise and criticism from others. You can end up being driven and perfectionistic because that's what gets applauded and affirmed. In the earlier days I didn't realize it, but I had a belief system behind my performance mentality: Work hard, be responsible, perform well, and people will love you. Work hard, be responsible, perform well, and God will love you.

We're often eager to listen to the voices that say, "Prove yourself, do something important, succeed, achieve" rather than God's voice, which whispers, "Rest in me; I am your shepherd. You don't have to prove anything. You are not an employee, you are my child."

But let's be honest. With all the pressure to succeed, even in ministry, it's hard to hear and really believe God's voice. For many of us, our activity is synonymous with our identity. It's how we convince ourselves we have value. To feel better about ourselves we work harder and longer and become prisoners of our own illusions.

Think for a moment about the times in Jesus' life when he heard God's audible voice. The first time God is recorded to have spoken words out of heaven in the life of Jesus was at his baptism.

> A voice from heaven said, "This is my Son, whom I love; with him I am well pleased."[1]

Notice what God said and didn't say. His words in that sacred moment "were neither directional (go here) nor instructional (do this). They were relational: This is my Son."[2]

This is on the very front end of Jesus' ministry. He hadn't preached a sermon, cast out a demon, healed a blind man, or raised somebody from the dead. These words were spoken over his obscure and hidden years. They had nothing to do with his performance. They had to do with sonship.

Based on my mental script, I might have expected God to say, "This is my employee, whom I have called. With him I am well pleased . . . if he performs well."

Even though Jesus was fully God, in his humanity I think he needed to hear the blessing and affirmation of his Father. That blessing of sonship became an anchor in his life. He would never play to the people to validate his significance. He would never try to draw a crowd to boost his ego. The anchor of blessedness allowed him to withstand the criticism of the Pharisees and not be swayed by the flattery of the multitudes.

The question is, Can we learn to tune out the fickle voices that for so long have dominated our lives? Can we listen to the voice of our Father who calls us his child?

Hear the blessing and voice of God in 1 John:

> See how very much our heavenly Father loves us, for he allows us to be called his children, and we really are![3]

There is no language of performance or achievement in that verse.

When you really get it, when you really understand how loved and blessed you are, the grip of approval addiction begins to loosen.

Hear the blessing and voice of God in Galatians:

> Now you are no longer a slave but God's own child. And since you are his child, everything he has belongs to you.[4]

Embracing our blessedness brings incredible freedom. We no longer live or die with the praise or criticism of others. We no longer have to frantically chase after significance. It takes the pressure off and delivers us from striving.

When you embrace your blessedness, you can echo these words of David:

> LORD, you have assigned me my portion and my cup;
> you have made my lot secure.
> The boundary lines have fallen for me in pleasant
>   places;
> surely I have a delightful inheritance.[5]

When you are a son, you can trust your good Father. In advance, he has assigned your portion and cup. When you are a son and you have a generous Father, your response is gratitude. And you can say "the boundary lines have fallen for me in pleasant places."

Because, no matter where the boundary lines fall, you are not an employee. You are a son.

When gratitude and sonship fills your heart, it spills over. Without competition or comparison or insecurity, we are free to bless others. We can tell them how much they matter to God. We don't have to turn the conversation to us, and we don't have to grab for the spotlight. We can allow others to succeed without envy because our identity isn't wrapped up in our achieving. We are God's children. And that is enough.

Questions for Discussion and Reflection

1. When the line gets blurred between your identity and ministry, what are the negative side effects?

2. If you operated purely out of your identity in Christ, how would it change you and your ministry?

3. Why is it hard for us to truly believe God loves us apart from our performance?

4. How does embracing your blessedness bring freedom?

twenty-one

DEATH TO DANCING BEARS

It was early Tuesday morning. We met in our usual hangout, an out-of-the-way coffee shop where we could talk openly and candidly away from the ears of church members. We met there many times, and we had shared a lot of life in that little spot. We were two pastors talking about our kids, marriages, hopes, joys, and frustrations with ministry.

On this day, when my friend walked through the door, we didn't exchange the usual banter. He was struggling, and I could see it. He'd recently taken a new position, but some of the familiar frustrations were returning. It had been a short honeymoon. He was becoming increasingly disenchanted with ministry.

"Sometimes as a worship pastor," he said, "I feel like a dancing bear. It's my job to get up and perform for the crowd, and as long as the performance is good, everyone is happy. Except me. Something is missing and I don't know what to do."

We spent the next couple of hours processing what was going

on inside him and some of the disillusionment he was feeling. I asked, "When do you feel most fulfilled?"

I was a bit surprised by his response: "I am most fulfilled when I get to sit down one-on-one with a person and walk away feeling like I actually pastored them."

Here was a guy with incredible talents and stage presence. He has led worship in some of the country's larger churches, and what was missing was his connection to people. His success had actually isolated him from the very congregation he was called to serve. He had moved from pastoring sheep to producing services.

I haven't been able to get that conversation out of my head. What my friend articulated, I have felt.

It reminds me of a brief conversation when my own words surprised me. One evening I walked in the door after a long day of meetings, and my wife matter-of-factly asked, "How was your day?"

"Today I felt more like the vice-president of a corporation than a pastor in a local church. I miss connecting with people in the church."

But the truth is, most days I was fine with it. People are a hassle. They are messy, frustrating, and often draining. It was easier (though less meaningful) to fill my days with running an organization.

Eugene Peterson said,

> Pastoral work consists of modest, daily, assigned work. It is like farm work. Most pastoral work involves routines similar to cleaning out the barn, mucking out the stalls, spreading manure, pulling weeds. This is not, any of it, bad work in itself, but if we expected to ride a glistening stallion in daily parades and then return to the barn where a lackey grooms our steed for us, we will be severely disappointed and end up being horribly resentful.[1]

He's so right. Over time, a subtle and incremental shift took place in my thinking about the work of pastoring. My focus shifted from ministering to people to managing them. I began to obsess about organizational development rather than people development. The wins began to be defined not by ministry to people but by the measurements of programs.

I began to view people as those we minister through rather than those we minister to. I know this is not an either/or proposition. There *are* both organizational and people sides to ministry. But my point is we need to lean into both aspects; we need to be good organizational leaders and yet we need to truly value and engage people.

I remember a season at Saddleback where we realized we couldn't hire everything done. Our appetite for new staff was voracious. So we decided the solution was in raising up volunteers. It became a full-court press to recruit and utilize them.

This seemed like a no-brainer. Of course we should be all about volunteers. But it wasn't going well. The staff complained they didn't have time to recruit volunteers, volunteers wouldn't follow through, and training was too time-consuming. In a "come to Jesus" meeting, we had to remind ourselves that volunteers weren't an interruption to ministry. *They were the ministry.* It's about people!

One of the valuable insights I learned from Rick Warren is about the priorities of a healthy church. They are

(1) Purposes of God
(2) People
(3) Programs
(4) Property

The order is crucial, and it dawned on me that we had switched numbers two and three. Our programs (ministries) had leapfrogged people in our priorities and focus.

Our intentions were noble. We hoped our programs were the means of discipling and growing people. But if we aren't careful, the planning, production, and participation become the focus, and the actual people the program was designed for get lost in the organizational grind.

Another factor fueling this problem is that programs are easy to measure. It's easy to count butts in seats, so that's usually what ends up getting celebrated. But the size of a church or ministry doesn't matter when it comes to caring for people. Some large churches are very personal and soft toward people. Some small churches are impersonal and hard toward people. It isn't about size, but mindset.

It also has nothing to do with role or position. Even if your primary responsibility is organizational or operational, you can still treat people with personal care and attention.

The words of the great English Puritan Richard Baxter, more than three hundred years ago, have never been more timely:

> The whole cause of our ministry must also be carried on in a tender love for our people. We must let them see that nothing pleases us more than what profits them. We should show them that what does them good does us good also. We should feel that nothing troubles us more than what hurts them.[2]

Questions for Discussion and Reflection

1. When are you the most fulfilled in your ministry?

2. Share a time when you were shown great personal care and attention. How did that impact you?

3. What are some practical steps you could take to raise the value of "people" in your ministry or church?

4. What helps you keep a focus on people?

DOES YOUR SOUL
HAVE A BACKBONE?

twenty-two

O ver the last few years my single most consistent prayer has been for spiritual courage. Being a coward comes quite naturally to me. I don't like to fight. I don't like rejection. I am definitely not a fan of pain. All of these are essential qualities of a coward.

Seriously, as I look in the rearview mirror at more than thirty years of ministry, one of my regrets has to do with this issue of courage. My fear of people leaving our church, my fear of people not liking me, my fear of criticism, and my fear of the "old guard" often kept me from making courageous leadership decisions. I could always justify my position in the name of "not going too fast" or "bringing people along" or "keeping unity," but the truth is, sometimes it was lack of courage. My courage often seemed to stumble over my propensity for people pleasing.

As I read Scripture and the history of the church, I am encouraged to see that God has used people who weren't naturally courageous. I believe Joshua was one of these. Joshua had been courageous as a younger man and later in life he is named by God as the successor to Moses.

For decades Moses had been the unquestioned leader of the people; his leadership was all they'd known. The Bible says he knew God "face to face," and that *"no one has ever shown the mighty power or performed the awesome deeds that Moses did in the sight of all Israel."*[1]

And now God comes to Joshua and says, "I want you to take *his* place." How intimidating would that be? No wonder God says "Be strong and courageous" six times!

It's interesting that Joshua was about to lead Israel into war, yet God doesn't talk strategy or tactics. He talks character. He talks courage. I think Erwin McManus is right:

> The history of God's people is not a record of God searching for courageous men and women who could handle the task, but God transforming the hearts of cowards.[2]

Courage is not an issue of wiring, but of willingness. It's not an issue of DNA, but of heart. I have always found comfort and hope in Ambrose Redmoon's definition:

> Courage is not the absence of fear, but rather the judgment that something else is more important than fear.[3]

In recent years my willingness to be courageous in spite of my fears has been tested. And, while I'm not the poster child for spiritual courage, God has been answering my prayer for it. In some difficult situations I haven't run. I've had the hard conversations. My people pleasing didn't win the day.

Looking back I realize there's a correlation between my communion *with* God and my courage *for* God. The deeper my intimacy, the greater my tenacity to stand courageously. The more Christ is my life, the less I need to find life in others' opinions.

As Martin Luther King Jr. began to receive threatening phone calls and letters, fear began to paralyze him. He had a defining moment one night with just him and God.

> It seemed as though I heard . . . an inner voice, saying "Stand up for righteousness, stand up for truth. God will be at your side forever." Almost at once my fears began to pass from me. . . . The outer situation remained the same, but God had given me inner calm.
>
> Three nights later, our home was bombed. Strangely enough, I accepted the word of the bombing calmly. My experience with God had given me new strength and trust. I know now that God is able to give us the interior resources to face the storms . . . of life.[4]

Let his words soak in. "My experience with God had given me new strength and trust." Abiding in the Vine[5] not only produces fruit, it makes us strong and courageous. I am also intrigued by King's statement that "God is able to give us interior resources to face the storm." It wasn't primarily the *cause* and the *community* that sparked courage, it was his *communion* with the Father.

As spiritual courage has begun to take root, I'm learning some key principles that help me in my quest to be courageous.

- What's the right thing to do? In the last few years, I have been disciplining myself to ask, "What's the *right* thing to do?" When faced with a situation where I'm tempted to do what's politically expedient, I am forcing myself to wrestle with this question. And most of the time I have a clear sense about what's right. Following through is not easy and there have been plenty of times I have wimped out.

Paul was very clear when he said, "Be careful to do what is right in the eyes of everybody."[6] Courage is like guardrails on a highway. You may not know where the road will twist and turn, but godly courage will keep you out of the ditches of sin and compromise and political expediency.

Erwin McManus gave a sharp insight: "We have to ask ourselves, 'Am I really trying to discern God's will, or determine whether I want to do it?' "[7]

- Separate decision making from problem solving. This principle was engrained in me through my service at Saddleback, and it's served me well since. I just wish I'd been aware of it twenty years earlier. When confronted with a difficult decision, we in ministry can let the fallout (problems) from it hijack us. I've been on teams where *everybody* knows the right choice, but the potential problems kept things stuck . . . sometimes for years.

I am by wiring more of a process thinker, and so I can quickly see potential problems, hurdles, and barriers. But, by separating decision making from problem solving, I don't let the problems cloud my ability to make the best decision. Once the best and right decision has been made, then we can dig in and start to problem solve.

- God is faithful. For most of my ministry, I knew this was true theologically, but in recent years I have found it to be true experientially. When I've done what I believed to be right and acted with spiritual courage, God has been faithful to show up with provision and presence. It hasn't been easy, but I am learning to really, deep down, trust him. In some ways, courage is a matter of trust. Do I trust that if I do what's right, he will have my back?

This doesn't mean everything will go smoothly just because I do what's right and live with courage. Look at the life of Joseph. He suffered for doing what was right; nevertheless, his trust in God carried him through dark and lonely days.

As Paul closes the book of 1 Corinthians he gives four imperatives that are as relevant today as they were in the first century.

Be on guard. Stand true to what you believe. Be courageous. Be strong.[8]

Questions for Discussion and Reflection

1. Who is the most courageous person you've known? How were they courageous?

2. How does our communion *with* God inform our courage *for* God?

3. What line or phrase from the Martin Luther King Jr. quote most inspires you? Why?

4. In our generation, what does it look like to do ministry "courageously"?

SUSTAINING A LIFETIME OF HEALTH

THE ART OF DOING NOTHING

I never thought I would be writing a chapter on Sabbath. For the first thirty years of my Christian life, the concept of Sabbath wasn't even a blip on my spiritual radar.

I never heard a sermon or read an article or book on the subject. I assumed it was one of those Old Testament things we just didn't do anymore. I lumped Sabbath into the same biblical category as the prohibition against wearing anything woven together with two kinds of material.[1]

Not only was Sabbath theologically irrelevant for me, it was practically irrelevant as well. I didn't know one person who practiced it. And my philosophy of ministry would have had no room for it. I have a "calling," and that calling demands sacrifice. Life is short; the needs are urgent. I have to squeeze all I can out of every second of every minute.

I totally bought into the "burn out for Jesus" mentality. When that's your mindset, there is no room for a theology of rest.

That prevalent mindset is very American, but very unbiblical. All my life, I've been taught how to go and go faster; no one ever taught me how to stop.

When I was six I got my very first bike at Christmas. It was a Vroom bicycle with motorcycle handlebars, and it made the sound of a motorcycle engine. There was just one problem. I didn't know how to ride a bike.

So, on a cold December day, my dad took me out to teach me. He walked alongside, holding the bike as I slowly learned to pedal and keep my balance. It wasn't long before my dad pointed the bike back toward the house and told me I was on my own.

Well, I did great until I arrived. I knew how to go, but I didn't know how to stop. I panicked and decided the only way to stop was to run into our car. As you can see, learning to stop is a lifelong problem for me.

In recent years I've begun to understand the importance of stopping and have begun to embrace a theology of rest. I have come to understand the importance of rhythm. We live in a universe defined by rhythm. As you inhale and exhale, your breathing has rhythm. Your heart beats in rhythm, and you have brainwaves that move in rhythm.

The seasons of the year are all about rhythm. Farming has a rhythm of planting, growing, and harvesting. The ocean waves have rhythm as the tide comes in and goes out. Even building muscle is marked by the rhythm of workout and recovery.

In fact, the reality of rhythm traces its roots all the way back to creation. After God completed his work, he rested on the seventh day.[2] He certainly did not rest because he was worn out from six straight days of creating. He rested to model rhythm.

This seventh day, the day of rest, was so important that God blessed it and declared it holy. The first thing the Bible ever declared holy was not an object or a place, but a "time," a twenty-four-hour period called Sabbath.

Just like the rest of the universe, you and I were made to live in rhythm. Recently I hiked my first "14er" (a 14,000-foot mountain peak) in Colorado. It was intense, tiring work. But once we got to the summit, we stopped, rested, relaxed, and took time to soak in the beauty surrounding us. Part of the reward of work is stopping long enough to see what's been accomplished.

That's a good picture of the rhythm God designed us to experience. Yes, life (and ministry) involves hard work. It's intense and tiring. But we must begin to learn that it's good to stop, rest, and take time to soak in the good gifts of God.

The world or your ministry may not give you permission to stop, but God does. In fact, he has commanded that we stop and rest.

In her practical book on Sabbath, Lynne Baab reminds us that Sabbath isn't about resting only when everything has been completed. "Sabbath is God's gracious 'five o'clock whistle' that gives me permission to stop and lay down my tools, ready or not."[3]

God's "top-ten list" included the command to observe the Sabbath. This is the longest of the Ten Commandments, with the most explanation attached to it. If we take seriously God's commands about adultery, coveting, stealing, lying, and idolatry, we also should take him seriously when it comes to practicing Sabbath.

Through missions work, I've spent a fair amount of time in the little African country of Malawi. Only about 3 percent of the population has access to electricity, so when the sun goes down, people head into their huts and are done for the day. A rhythm of work and rest comes naturally.

With the advent and availability of technology, sunset is no longer a boundary for us. We can work around the clock. We can stay plugged in and engaged 24/7. But just because we can doesn't mean we should.

Our love for speed and our obsession with doing more has led to an addiction that knows nothing of rhythm. Wayne Muller diagnoses our culture accurately:

> We have forgotten what enough feels like. We live in a world seduced by its own unlimited potential.[4]

My own addiction to speed and noise and productivity has made the practice of Sabbath incredibly challenging. Who knew "doing nothing" could be so hard?

When I first started trying to practice Sabbath, I hated it. It was not enjoyable or spiritual. It felt like de-tox. I kept wanting to check e-mail or work on a ministry project or whittle down my to-do list. I was so driven and overloaded that slowing down actually felt uncomfortable. And even when my body was still, internally I was still amped.

Over time I've learned that Sabbath is not a have-to, it's a *get-to*. This incredible gift from God allows us to reflect, restore, replenish. During Sabbath God whispers, "I'm in control. The world can get along without you for twenty-four hours." We are not as indispensable as we think.

When I practice Sabbath I find that I'm more *present*. I tend to do a better job of living in the moment and enjoying life's simple pleasures. I notice the beauty of creation more easily. I listen a little better, and I feel more joyful.

Practicing Sabbath is like getting a weekly perspective adjustment. When I stop and reflect and pray and spend time with God, I'm reminded of what's most important.

Living in the twenty-first century is like being in a jar of muddy river water. Only when the jar remains *still* will the sediment drop to the bottom and the water once again become clear. Sabbath keeping helps me see God and life more clearly.

Through Sabbath I am learning that my significance is not wrapped up in my productivity. On Sabbath, I am not Lance the pastor, Lance the leader, Lance the financial provider, or Lance the Replenish guy. I am simply a beloved son.

I love Pete Scazzero's template for practicing Sabbath—Stop, Rest, Delight, and Contemplate.[5]

- *Stop.* Put productivity on hold for twenty-four hours.
- *Rest.* For some of us the most spiritual thing we can do is take a nap.
- *Delight.* Isaiah 58 talks about enjoying and delighting in Sabbath.[6] Sabbath is a day to enjoy what God has created.
- *Contemplate.* Take time to "be" with God. The seventh day is a Sabbath "to the Lord."[7]

Maybe as you consider the practice of Sabbath, you're filled with questions about how this would look practically. Or maybe in light of your season of life or responsibilities, the practice of Sabbath feels unrealistic. I want to challenge you to wrestle with this biblically and then have some serious conversation with your family or ministry team about developing a healthy rhythm.

I don't know exactly what it will look like for you, but Sabbath is helping me become a better Christ follower and a better person.

Questions for Discussion and Reflection

1. In the past, what has been your view of Sabbath?

2. What would be your biggest barriers to practicing Sabbath consistently?

3. Sabbath is to include "delight." It's a day to enjoy what God has created. What could you do on Sabbath that brings you delight and is life-giving to you?

4. How is Sabbath different than "a day off"?

twenty-four

SAY YES BY SAYING NO

T ony Blair, former British Prime Minister, once said, "The art of leadership is not saying yes, it is saying no." His insight is not only true about people who lead organizations and nations and churches; it's also true of people who lead themselves well.

But learning to say no is easier said than done, especially for those of us in ministry. With so many opportunities, so many ideas, so much vision, and so many needs, deciding when to say yes and when to say no has never been harder.

Everywhere you go these days people are overloaded with, and sometimes paralyzed by, choices. Not only is the number increasing, but the speed at which choices are coming at us also is accelerating. We suffer from option overload. The average grocery store carries more than thirty thousand products. In *The Paradox of Choice*, Barry Schwarz writes about our option overload.

> Scanning the shelves of my local supermarket recently, I found 85 different varieties of crackers. . . . [N]ext to the crackers were 285 varieties of cookies. Among chocolate chip

cookies, there were 21 options. Among Goldfish, there were 20 different varieties to choose from.[1]

I feel option overload every time I eat at The Cheesecake Factory. Their menu is just a tad shorter than *War and Peace*. The last time I was there, the waitress said there were also a few specials that weren't on the menu! Unbelievable. This tidal wave of options often leaves us feeling paralyzed. When I say yes to one entrée, I see that I'm saying no to hundreds of other good choices.

In ministry, every week we are handed a menu for how we will spend our time. The options seem ten times the number they used to be. The exponential growth of conferences, parachurch ministries, technology, mission opportunities, family problems, and community needs can leave me paralyzed in deciding where I should give my time.

Amidst an external explosion of options, there's also an internal dynamic at work. For many of us, internally we feel pressure to say yes to everyone and everything. We think we should say yes to everyone who has a ministry idea. We think we should say yes to everyone who requests our time. From my own journey, I can tell you that part of this is driven by motives to serve God and help people.

However, some internal pressure comes from my own poor boundaries and insecurities. If I'm honest, many times the yes in ministry hasn't been motivated by servanthood, but rather by insecurity.

I suffer from what I affectionately refer to as "terminal niceness." I don't want to disappoint anyone. I don't want anyone to feel let down by their pastor. It's unrealistic to try keeping everyone satisfied, but I've spent years trying. This is a symptom of being an approval junkie.

Such codependency leads to dysfunction in a church and takes a huge personal toll; the result is cluttered churches and cluttered lives. It might not be a bad idea for us who lead to stand in front of our mirror and practice saying *no* over and over. It feels so counterintuitive to say no to good opportunities and legitimate needs.

What I'm finally learning is that saying no isn't unspiritual or uncaring. As William Ury says, "Like all good No's, ours were in service to a higher Yes."[2]

If I'm going to navigate the tsunami of options and choices and demands of ministry, I must discover the "higher Yes." Until I discover the "higher Yes," I will always be the slave of urgent needs and pleasing people.

Imagine your life as a tree. The roots are what you fundamentally value; they are your core convictions, your deeper Yes. The branches and the fruit are what you deeply want to experience, the life you want to live; these are your delightful Yes.

The narrow trunk that connects the two together is a defined No. The trunk is the least attractive. It's the narrowest part of the tree. It has the thickest skin of anyplace on the tree. But it is the carrier of life from the roots to the fruit.

Consider the example of Jesus. After a busy day of ministry the day before, he gets up before anyone else. He heads out to a solitary place where he can be alone with his Father. The disciples find him and say, "Everyone is looking for you." Music to the ears of codependent ministry leaders. The feeling of being in demand can be intoxicating.

Notice Jesus' response to the clamoring of the people: *no.* Instead he says, "Let's go somewhere else."[3] Though the passage doesn't say so specifically, it seems clear the higher Yes came out of his prayer time. His solitude clarified the yes and defined the no.

Later we find Jesus again going out at daybreak to a solitary place. When the people caught up with him, the Bible says, "They tried to keep him from leaving them." But again his answer was no. He told them, essentially, "I must preach the good news of God's kingdom to the other towns also—that's why I was sent."[4]

Maybe part of the reason we have such a hard time with no is that we aren't still long enough to discover the yes. Think about it. This would be a great exercise on a personal retreat. Ask yourself, "What is the higher Yes in my life that will become the filter through which I make decisions?" Write it down and declare it to those around you.

The only way to have the courage to say no is to turn your values into resolve. Drive a stake in the ground and determine that you will not be driven by the fickle opinions of others. If you wait until you're in the moment, you will cave in. By deciding your "higher Yes," you are essentially pre-deciding when you will say no.

When you're navigating all the options and choices in front of you, pay attention to your gut instincts. Listen to your emotions. William Ury gives us solid advice:

> Treat your emotions as signposts, pointing at your core needs. Rather than being your enemy, your emotions can become your ally, for they can help you uncover your yes.[5]

One word of caution. As you stand up for what matters to you, do it in a way that doesn't destroy relationships in the process. Make sure your no is not just right, but also respectful and gracious.

I remember Chip Ingram talking about a request he'd made to Chuck Swindoll to endorse Chip's latest book. Chip said he received back the nicest, kindest, most gracious rejection letter he had ever received.

Always treat others with the dignity they deserve as people who matter to God and are created in his image. But have the courage to say no to some things so you can say yes to the best things.

Questions for Discussion and Reflection

1. What has been your journey with learning to say no? Do you still struggle with saying no?

2. Where, specifically, do you find it difficult to say no?

3. Is there something in your life or ministry you should say no to and stop doing?

4. What is the "higher Yes" in your life that should become the filter through which you make decisions?

twenty-five

NOISE-CANCELING HEADPHONES FOR THE SOUL

I was flying from Charlotte to San Francisco. Two rambunctious children were in my row. Their parents, up in first class, sipped wine while I babysat in the cheap seats.

To make matters worse, across the aisle was a toddler who cried for the first two thousand miles. This trip had stress and frustration written all over it. To save the day I reached for my trusted travel companion: noise-canceling Bose headphones. As I pulled them out of the case I could almost hear the "Hallelujah Chorus." They offered the hope of escape and sanity, no matter what surrounded me.

If I'm going to be spiritually healthy, I must find ways to cancel the noise around me and experience times of solitude. *Solitude.* The word itself sounds serene and peaceful. Most everyone I know longs for more solitude.

In the biblical stories we discover that many God moments came when people were alone in his presence (e.g., Abraham, Moses,

David, Jesus, Paul). When Moses went up on the mountain to meet with God, it wasn't until the seventh day that God spoke.[1]

Intuitively we know it's important to have extended time alone. But experientially it feels elusive, and this reality sets up a titanic clash of two worlds.

On one hand is the world of the inner man, needing soul connection with God. Words that characterize this world, when healthy, are words like *time, reflection, quiet, depth,* and *slow.*

On the other hand is the outer, or external, visible world. Words that characterize this world are words like *fast, instant, convenient, fragmented, noisy, shallow,* and *exhausted.*

Here is a portion of a journal entry regarding my own struggle with this issue.

> Lord, I confess to you that it's hard for me to be quiet and silent. I want to hear your voice, but my world is filled with so much noise that I usually miss your gentle nudges. The flurry of activity in my life drowns out your voice. I feel disconnected. I don't fully understand why it is so difficult to be still and rest in you. I often feel like a rubber band that is stretched too tightly.
>
> I'm sure the diagnosis involves taking a hard look at my drivenness and performance mentality. I also know that I need to own this. I am not a victim of circumstance or situation. My lack of solitude is a reflection of choices that I make. I just want to tell you that I need you and desire to change this area of my life. Help it to be enough just to be with you.

We are conditioned to surround ourselves with noise. With our incessant activity, frenetic pace, and electronic leashes, it's no wonder silence and solitude are rare commodities. We despise "dead time."

Too much noise and too much activity can be toxic to the soul. When you go to the doctor and discover you have an infection, one of the first things you hear is "get some rest." Just like your body needs time to recover from an infection, your soul needs time to recover from the push and pull of twenty-first-century ministry life.

Again, solitude feels counterintuitive to the way most of us do ministry. Solitude

- requires being present when we're used to being productive.
- requires listening when we're used to talking.
- requires quiet when we're used to noise.
- requires stillness when we're used to busyness.
- requires going internal when we're used to going external.
- requires facing who we are when we're used to projecting who we want people to think we are.

In stark contrast to our ministry rhythm today is the rhythm of Jesus' life. Once, while doing ministry in Capernaum, "after sunset the people brought to Jesus all the sick and demon-possessed." In fact, the "whole town gathered" at his door.[2] Talk about a demanding day of ministry.

The next morning, "while it was still dark, Jesus got up [and] left the house."[3] We *expect* him to get up before dark to begin another busy day. After all, he's God, and there's much to do.

He only has three years of public ministry—not much time to start a movement that will turn the world upside down. You'd think his strategy would be to push hard for three years. Travel as much as possible, see as many people as possible, preach as many times as possible, develop an organizational plan, and raise up as many leaders as possible.

Yet when Jesus left the house that morning, he didn't head out to do ministry. He went to a solitary place to be alone with his Father.

As you walk through the Gospels, you discover that the thread of solitude runs consistently through the life of Jesus. At the beginning of his ministry, he goes off for an extended time of fasting and prayer. After he hears of the death of John the Baptist, he gets in a boat and goes off to a solitary place. When he's about to choose his disciples, he goes off to be alone with the Father.

Solitude is not so much about a place as it is about space—space to reflect, pray, think, listen, and *be*.

Thomas Moore has written,

> The vessel in which soul-making takes place is an inner container scooped out by reflection and wonder.[4]

Imagine your life as a container. It's filled with possessions, pressures, distractions, responsibility, and fast-paced living. Moore says that it's reflection and wonder (solitude) that scoop these out of our soul. Through solitude there will be room in your soul for you to meet God and for him to do the work in you that he longs to do.

Your life does not have an infinite capacity. Solitude creates capacity for God.

Learning solitude has been a struggle for me. I resonate with Gary Thomas's words: "We who have been drugged by diversions cannot expect to enter the quiet without a struggle. Our souls will roar for diversion."[5]

In recent years, as I've been learning to practice solitude, the greatest impact has to do with the word "freedom."

Henri Nouwen eloquently articulated the freedom that solitude can bring:

> [Solitude] is the place where Christ remodels us in his own image and frees us from the victimizing compulsions of the world.[6] . . . In solitude we become aware that our worth is not the same as our usefulness.[7]

Extended times of solitude and reflection and prayer are beginning to loosen the grip of my distorted thinking. I'm starting to get free from the seduction of believing that productivity equals importance and that busyness equals significance.

Psalm 131 expresses the destination where solitude is taking me.

> My heart is not proud, O LORD, my eyes are not haughty; I do not concern myself with great matters or things too wonderful for me. But I have stilled and quieted my soul; like a weaned child with its mother, like a weaned child is my soul within me.[8]

David describes a picture of total and absolute contentment. No frantic pushing. No compulsive striving. Just a stilled and quieted soul. That is what solitude offers.

Questions for Discussion and Reflection

1. When you hear the word *solitude*, what images come to mind? Are you drawn to solitude, or are you repelled by the idea of being alone?

2. Which of the "Solitude requires . . ." bullet points in this chapter most connect with you? Why? Which make you the most uncomfortable? Why?

3. If you could sneak away for an afternoon of solitude, where would you go?

4. Henri Nouwen said solitude "is the place where Christ remodels us in his own image and frees us from the victimizing compulsions of the world." Unpack his statement. What does he mean?

twenty-six

THE MOST EMBARRASSING GAP IN MY LEADERSHIP

I really didn't want to write this chapter. But I know you can't talk about spiritual health without talking about this topic. In the past, when I preached about it or wrote about it, I always felt a gnawing inadequacy. If you were to chart my ministry and spiritual journey, there would be large gaps where this spiritual practice has been missing in action.

So, let me shoot straight with you. I struggle with my prayer life. When I hear guys like Jim Cymbala and read about prayer in his church at Brooklyn Tabernacle, I am both inspired and depressed all at the same time.

I know that too often I've relied only on plans, strategies, skills, and methods to build the ministry. When you're a leader, you have a bent toward action, toward doing. And that's where you get your strokes and sense of significance. Prayer places value on waiting, seeking, listening, and discerning. I know it's not true theologically, but prayer has often felt passive.

While my prayer life is still not what I want it to be, it's much different than it used to be. I remember the day my prayer life began to change. It was a Thursday. I know it was a Thursday because that's when our church bulletin got printed.

I was sitting at my desk reading a passage of Scripture I'd read dozens of times before. It was the story of Jesus cleansing the temple.

It's a stunning scene. I have this picture of the disciples standing with their mouths open, their eyes as big as saucers. I can see a couple of them thinking, *Isn't this a bit of an overreaction?* Maybe one says to another, "This is not going to help his popularity." Maybe Judas is embarrassed that Jesus is making such a big scene.

Picture this moment. Jesus marches in like he owns the place (and he does, but they don't know it). He starts flipping tables and grabbing people by the collar, saying they can't bring their merchandise through the temple. He gets into their faces and tells them to get out.

What happened to Jesus meek and mild? Why was he so ticked off? His house was being prostituted for purposes other than what he intended.

As feathers flew and coins clattered, the calm turned to chaos. Jesus angrily chastises them and basically says, "This place looks and feels more like a mall than a temple. There is more emphasis on purchases than on prayer."[1]

Each of the merchants would have vigorously defended his own right to be there. Actually, they were offering a legitimate service of providing animals for the sacrifices.

The moneychangers would also have defended their place in the temple. When people came to pay their temple tax, they had to use coins minted in Jerusalem. They needed someplace to exchange their foreign currency. But the merchants were tacking on big-time surcharges and turning the temple into a profit-making machine.

The first-century merchants and moneychangers were in the

temple, but they didn't have the spirit of the temple. The emphasis was on profit margin, not prayer meetings. The priority had become financial transaction rather than spiritual transformation.

Interestingly, Jesus "would not allow anyone to carry merchandise through the temple courts."[2] All their activity was violating the space that had been reserved for people to meet with God. The primary had been overrun by the secondary.

Jesus rebukes them and says the reputation of God's house should be one of prayer. *The heartbeat of a God-centered and healthy ministry is the heartbeat of prayer.*

Notice that Jesus did not say this is primarily to be a house of preaching or teaching. Or worship, or ministry, or programs.

The Holy Spirit drew my focus to Jesus' words, "My house will be called a house of prayer for all nations."[3] I picked up the church bulletin lying on the corner of my desk. I thumbed through it and noticed how many things we had going on. It was chock full of opportunities, classes, and events. We were a full-service church and proud of it. But I remember thinking, *No one would ever accuse us of being a house of prayer.*

The Holy Spirit took the spotlight and shined it on my own life. My next thought pierced my spirit: *and no one would ever accuse me of being a man of prayer.* I repented. I knew something had to change.

I really had no idea how to change my impotent and sporadic prayer life. So I started reading books on prayer. As I read some of the classics as well as some contemporary authors, I was inspired and challenged. Little by little God began to intensify my desire. As I now look back on those days, I would tell you I read my way into a greater passion for prayer.

Proverbs says, "He who walks with the wise grows wise."[4] As I read these great works, in a way I was walking with the wise, people who were wise in the ways of prayer. As a result, I was growing wise in the ways of prayer.

During this season of change, I also began to notice how different the prayers of the Bible were from the prayers we prayed in my church. Either personally or with your team, you might want to spend some time looking at Paul's prayers in Ephesians 3:14–21 and Colossians 1:9–14.

As God was rewiring my heart I knew I also needed to make some changes externally for prayer to become a priority in my life and ministry. So I began to structure prayer into my schedule with far more intentionality than ever before. I created a system that would modify my behavior and reinforce what God was doing in my heart.

I blocked time to be in our church's prayer room. We structured prayer as a priority in our staff meeting rather than simply tacking it on at the beginning or end of the meeting. I developed a personal prayer team from a group of trusted individuals who interceded very personally on my behalf. I met biweekly during lunch with them so we could pray together. We also started prayer walking our city and having occasional nights of prayer for our small groups.

I don't know how it looks for you to structure prayer into your world, but I do know that structuring these pieces into my weekly schedule made a huge difference in my passion for prayer. The most important thing was creating space in my week for me to be with God.

Over time prayer has become more natural. It has become less transactional and more relational. It's the difference between a kid asking his dad for something and a couple sharing their innermost beings with each other. As I put more focus on pursuing Jesus than pursuing my ministry, prayer is a thread that weaves its way throughout my day. It is frequent connection and communion with the One who matters most to me.

Questions for Discussion and Reflection

1. Jesus said, "My house will be called a house of prayer." He wanted his house to have that reputation. What's your ministry's reputation? What are you known for?

2. How would you describe your own journey with prayer? How would you describe your prayer life over the last three months?

3. For you personally, what tends to crowd out prayer in your life?

4. For your ministry, what could you do to make prayer a greater priority?

HUMILITY AND HUBRIS

I have been sitting and staring at a blank computer screen for a while now. It's more than writer's block. I am conflicted.

I know I can't write about matters of the soul and not discuss the quality of humility. But I also know myself, and how much pride has been and is in my life. It's been a constant companion for more than fifty years. I am well acquainted with the dark side of leadership.

Not long ago I read through Andrew Murray's short work called *Humility*. In processing his writing, I was struck by two contrasting realities. First I was reminded how prevalent humility was in the life and teachings of Jesus. His very first words in the Sermon on the Mount are about those who are poor (humble) in spirit. And the Cross is the ultimate manifesto on humility.

Second, I was rebuked by how little we preach and practice humility today. When is the last time you read a blog, sat in a conference session, or heard a sermon on humility?

Murray says, "If humility be the secret of His atonement, then the health and strength of our spiritual life will entirely depend on putting this grace first too."[1] Notice he doesn't say anything about the size of your ministry or breadth of your influence. He does say the "health and strength" of your spiritual life is tied to a spirit of humility.

Maturing as a leader comes with some hard but rich lessons. One of those is to learn that real joy comes not in promoting self but dying to self. And, that real satisfaction comes in being nothing so that Jesus might be everything.

One night John and Margaret Maxwell hosted a dinner for a group of executive pastors from around the country. At the end of the evening John shared a little about some of his latest thinking. It was largely about humility.

He pointed out that people with leadership gifts have an advantage. They see things before other people. They can size up a situation more quickly than others. They often are quickest to figure out what needs to be done. They have an advantage. But John pointed out that humble leaders, godly leaders, do not take advantage of their advantage. They don't manipulate; they don't self-promote.

We need more ministry heroes who are as Jesus described himself: "gentle and humble in heart."[2] There is a subtle but inherent danger for leaders that impacts our humility. We have been given a gift from God to inspire people, catalyze movement, and foster momentum. People respond, and things get done, and people follow "you." That can mess with both your head and your heart. We can begin to think it's because of us and about us.

We can obsess with success and forget that what draws a crowd isn't necessarily what draws God. We forget that he cares just as much about the means as he does the ends. We don't mean for it to happen, but we become spiritually disoriented.

The more fruitfulness and success we experience, the greater the temptation. Your success and the praise that follows it will be a test of your humility. Jim Collins' research validates this truth. In *How the Mighty Fall*, he identifies the first stage of decline as "hubris born of success."

> Stage 1 kicks in when people become arrogant, regarding success virtually as an entitlement, and they lose sight of the true underlying factors that created success in the first place.[3]

Those words ring true for ministry leaders as much as CEOs of secular corporations.

When hubris begins to win the day in a ministry, there are some telltale signs.

- It's more about the leader's vision than it is about Jesus.
- Prayer is conspicuously absent.
- Achieving the cause gets more attention than abiding in Christ.
- There's a utilitarian view of people.
- There's a spirit of competition and comparing.

In contrast, here are some practical means by which we can embrace humility:

- Make much of Jesus. Speak of him often. As you share vision, always point people back to Jesus. As John the Baptist said, *"He must become greater and greater, and I must become less and less."*[4]
- Regularly remind yourself that the church is not "your" church and that the ministry you serve is not "your" ministry. We are shepherds and stewards; Jesus is the owner.
- Work hard at praising others and not yourself. The challenge from Solomon is direct and straightforward: *Don't praise yourself; let others do it!*[5] Pay attention to those inner promptings when the Holy Spirit is spotlighting self-promotion.

- Be interested in others more and interested in yourself less. Ask people questions about their lives. Get someone to tell you their story.
- Stay in touch with grace. Never get over what it means that God loves you and saved you and adopted you into his family. Rewind. Let that soak in for a moment. The eternal God, the Creator, chose you.
- Enlist a pride patrol. Ask a couple people you trust to help you. When they see hints of posturing or self-promotion, don't just give them permission to come to you—insist that they come to you. By helping you see blind spots they will help you be a more godly leader and potentially avert a train wreck in your life.

Whenever the topic of humility comes up, I think of Pastor Joseph. I wish you could meet him. He pastors a small church in the small African country of Malawi. There are about seventy-five people who meet in a mud hut they call "church."

Pastor Joseph has an infectious enthusiasm for Jesus, and he cares deeply about his community. He started a brick-making business and trains the women of his village how to raise a garden. His little congregation operates a school for about 250 children. He and his wife have taken in twenty-three AIDS orphans to live with them.

Pastor Joseph will never write a book. He likely will never speak at a conference. He'll probably never travel more than just a few miles from his home. He will never be famous in this world. But his life is deeply centered in Jesus . . . and that's enough.

Questions for Discussion and Reflection

1. Why do you think we hear little preaching and teaching about humility today?

2. Who has been an example of humility to you? What do you notice in their life that is evidence of humility?

3. John Maxwell said that godly leaders don't take advantage of their advantage. What does that mean for you and how you do ministry?

4. Which of the five signs of hubris listed in this chapter do you and your ministry need to be careful about?

twenty-eight

STAY IN TOUCH WITH YOUR DARK SIDE

D*epravity* is a word we don't use much anymore. It feels old school and has a sharp, indicting edge.

We've worked hard to soften the sharp edges of faith. We tend to focus on what people can be rather than what they are and were. We talk a lot about life change and transformation, but rarely about our depravity and darkness of heart.

I really believe part of what it means to be spiritually healthy is to avoid losing touch with one's own depravity. I must hold in balance my blessedness and brokenness. Yes, I am more blessed than I can even fathom, but I am also more broken than I can grasp. Even though I've been redeemed and the "old man" has been crucified, I still live in a fallen world and the seduction of the flesh is still an everyday battle.

I have been a Christ-follower about forty years. I've been in ministry about thirty, and yet I'm amazed and ashamed at how dark my heart can be. I'm astounded by how easily I still can be drawn to lust, or greed, or slander, or dishonesty, or prejudice.

Over the last five years, I've read a lot of classics on spiritual formation. One of the glaring distinctions between these older writings and contemporary Christian literature has to do with this issue of depravity. The spiritual giants that have come before us had a much greater awareness of their depravity, and they often wrote about it.

They seemed to be more in touch with what they were capable of and, as a result, they didn't trust themselves. We hear a lot today about self-discovery, leveraging our strengths and maximizing our potential. But I need to realize my potential isn't all positive. I have the potential to destroy my marriage. I have the potential to divide a church. I have the potential to bring disgrace to the name of Jesus.

God has a long history of reminding his people of their brokenness.

There's an interesting pattern that develops in Deuteronomy when God is speaking to the Israelites. Five different times he calls on them to remember they'd been slaves in Egypt and he had rescued them. Then, each time he gives them a command to follow. But the starting place was for them to recall what they had been.

> *Remember that you were slaves in Egypt . . .* now, observe the Sabbath.
> *Remember that you were slaves in Egypt . . .* now, when you release a slave, supply him liberally.
> *Remember that you were slaves in Egypt . . .* now, give a freewill offering.
> *Remember that you were slaves in Egypt . . .* now, treat foreigners, orphans, and widows fairly.
> *Remember that you were slaves in Egypt . . .* now, when you harvest, leave some behind for the foreigner, orphan, and widow.[1]

Then, the Lord says,

> *Remember this and never forget how you provoked the LORD*

your God to anger in the desert. From the day you left Egypt until you arrived here, you have been rebellious against the LORD.[2]

I'm struck by the phrase "Remember this and never forget." Never forget what you're capable of. Never forget how easily you can rebel. Never forget your potential for evil.

When Isaiah saw the Lord in all his glorious majesty, his immediate response was to see and feel his own depravity: "Woe to me . . . I am ruined!"[3] But, here's the good news. God doesn't send him away or rebuke him. He sends an angel to purify and cleanse him. And then God commissions him to go and be his representative to the people.

God is not surprised or put off by my depravity. He can still use me in spite of what lurks in my heart.

Over the last few years I've done a couple of extended fasts. When people find out you've done a long fast, they're curious about what happened. They always want to know if you received significant revelation from God or got clear direction about a major life decision.

They're usually disappointed with my answer. The single most significant spiritual outcome of these two fasts had to do with depravity. During my fasts God put me up on the operating table and did spiritual surgery. He shined the light on broken areas and went to work on them. And, even though it was sobering and painful, it was good and helpful.

Staying in touch with my depravity helps foster humility and nurture dependence. François Fénelon said,

> The closer you get to God, the more miserable things you will find in your heart. This is not a negative thing—God allows it to let you lose confidence in yourself. You will have accomplished something when you can look at your inner corruptness without anxiety or discouragement and simply trust in God.[4]

I've also found that being aware of my depravity makes me want to pursue accountability. Every godly leader knows you can't trust yourself. When I see the darkness of my heart, I'm painfully aware of how much I need checks and balances.

I need people in my life asking me the hard questions. I need people who fully know me. They know the good, the bad, *and* the ugly, and they love me anyway. But they're not afraid to hold me to a standard of godly leadership.

Another benefit of staying in touch with my depravity is that it helps me be less critical and more loving toward people. At least for me, the more I have pondered my brokenness and the wonder of God's grace toward me, the more I tend to see people differently and treat them a little more graciously. When I know what's inside me, who am I to be condescending or stand in harsh judgment over anyone?

Occasionally you'll hear someone talk about "owning your stuff." It's all about taking responsibility and refusing to live in denial. It's about being honest. I think it's time for us in ministry to own our stuff: take responsibility, acknowledge our depravity, and be honest about the darkness that still lives inside us. We will be healthier for it.

Questions for Discussion and Reflection

1. How would you define the word *depravity*? What was taught about depravity in churches you've attended?

2. The Lord said, "Remember this and never forget how you provoked the LORD your God to anger in the desert. From the day you left Egypt until you arrived here, you have been rebellious against the LORD." Why did he want Israel to remember how they had provoked him to anger?

3. In your opinion, is it helpful to stay in touch with your dark side? If so, how?

4. In this chapter, the statement was made that "being aware of my depravity makes me want to pursue accountability." Why would this be true?

twenty-nine

A VALUABLE LESSON FROM ALCOHOLICS ANONYMOUS

Taking an exam, whether medical or academic, is no fun. When the doctor asks you to climb up on the exam table, you know it won't be a pleasant experience. But we know it's necessary if we're going to be helped. And whether it's a test in school or a doctor's exam, the goal is the same: to assess reality and to get an accurate picture of what *is*. A proper diagnosis is a prerequisite to proper treatment.

In the generations before us, believers practiced something called self-examination (sometimes referred to as "the examen of conscience"). This was the practice of getting up on the spiritual examination table and letting the Holy Spirit probe and prod and accurately diagnose your soul's condition.

It seems to me most Christians treat spiritual self-examination like I treat going to the doctor or dentist. I know I need to go. I know I need regular visits for sustained health. But I can easily talk myself into canceling my appointment because I'm too busy or something more urgent has come up. The truth is, it's just easier not to go, and I can always justify not going.

I can have the same reaction to spiritual self-examination. There are always more pressing matters to attend to. Yet, in generations past, many serious Christ followers made this a regular practice.

Jonathan Edwards, the famed eighteenth-century pastor, wrote seventy statements—guiding principles—that would steer his entire life. At the time he started writing these guiding principles, he'd been a Christian only about a year and was eighteen years old.

These "Resolutions," as they were called, were Edwards' attempt to discipline himself for the purpose of godliness; he would use them as the basis for practicing self-examination. The Resolutions covered not only his pursuit of God but also how he spent his time, managed his relationships, took care of himself physically, and aimed to live a life of no regret.

He committed to asking the Holy Spirit to search his heart and help him keep to his resolutions, vowing to review them weekly for the rest of his life as a kind of soul maintenance. He was so intentional about self-examination that he built it into the very fabric of his resolutions—for example, about how he would handle sin in his life.

> *Resolved, whenever I do any conspicuously evil action, to trace it back, till I come to the original cause.*[1]

In other words, he would place his sin on the examination table and, with the Spirit's help, trace it back to where it started. Often behind the act of my sin is a deeper brokenness; Edwards knew the value of examining the *why* behind the *what*.

In *The Unwavering Resolve of Jonathan Edwards,* Steven Lawson writes about his tenacity.

> When he discovered sin in his life, Edwards felt compelled to trace it to its origin—the heart. Mere behavior modification

wasn't enough. . . . In order to become holy he must trace the waters of sin upstream until he reached the springs from which the iniquity flowed—his motives.[2]

In contemporary times, Alcoholics Anonymous and other recovery groups have grasped and applied the power of examination. The Fourth AA Step reads, "[We] made a searching and fearless moral inventory of ourselves."

My friend John Baker, founder of Celebrate Recovery, has put his finger on at least one factor in my own aversion to self-examination.

> When you clean out a closet, you uncover things that may have been stuffed in a dark corner for years. That stuff may even be stinking up your house. But you've ignored it because the thought of closet cleaning is just too overwhelming.[3]

At the core, examination of self is difficult because of my love of self. Self-love exaggerates my virtues and minimizes my sin. And, examination brings my self-love out into the light.

Self-examination is like reconciling my bank statement—its condition is never as good as I thought it was. I always tend to think I've spent less than I have, and I tend to think I have more money than I actually do. Reconciling my account helps me have an accurate picture of my financial reality.

One reason self-examination is so crucial is found in the words of Jeremiah: "The heart is deceitful above all things and beyond cure. Who can understand it?"[4]

Because this is true, the Holy Spirit must do the examination. Reflective practices are the hardest. The eye can see everything but itself. In the same way, it's easy for me to see the disease and dysfunction in others but give myself a clean bill of health.

François Fénelon said, "God is able to seek out and destroy the roots of self-love. You, on your own, could never find those hidden roots."[5] And Solomon wrote, "The lamp of the LORD searches the spirit of a man; it searches out his inmost being."[6]

If you're a parent, you know the challenges of taking your kids to the doctor. One is getting your child to stay still long enough to be examined. Many of us have the same challenge with self-examination. Our lives are so full and so noisy we can't seem to be still long enough to let the Holy Spirit really take a look at what's happening inside.

As a starting point, let me challenge you this week to set aside just a half hour for self-examination. Ask the Holy Spirit to reveal what you need to see. Consider using the following questions that John Wesley used in this practice.

- Am I consciously or unconsciously creating the impression that I'm better than I really am? In other words, am I a hypocrite?
- Am I honest in all my acts and words, or do I exaggerate?
- Do I confidentially pass on to another what was told to me in confidence?
- Can I be trusted?
- Am I a slave to dress, friends, work, or habits?
- When did I last speak to someone else about my faith?
- Do I pray about the money I spend?
- Do I get to bed on time and get up on time?
- Do I disobey God in anything?
- Am I jealous, impure, critical, irritable, touchy, or distrustful?
- Is there anyone I fear, dislike, disown, criticize, hold a resentment toward, or disregard? If so, what am I doing about it?

Search me, O God, and know my heart; test me and know my anxious thoughts. Point out anything in me that offends you, and lead me along the path of everlasting life.[7]

Questions for Discussion and Reflection

1. What is the benefit of self-examination as described in this chapter?

2. If you were going to develop a set of resolutions to review every week, what would be a couple that made your list? (These could be how you spend time, manage your relationships, take care of yourself physically, etc.)

3. Why is the Holy Spirit's role so important in the practice of self-examination?

4. Is this a practice you should try to engage in? If so, what would that look like?

thirty

PRACTICING THE
PRESENCE OF PEOPLE

Tucked away in the Old Testament book of Exodus is a vivid picture of God's heart for people. God wanted to make sure his priests never disconnected serving him from loving others. These verses are a timely challenge to all of us who lead in ministry.

> Whenever Aaron enters the Holy Place, he will bear the names of the sons of Israel over his heart on the breastpiece of decision as a continuing memorial before the LORD. Also put the Urim and the Thummim in the breastpiece, so they may be over Aaron's heart whenever he enters the presence of the LORD. Thus Aaron will always bear the means of making decisions for the Israelites over his heart before the LORD.[1]

Whenever Aaron performed his priestly duties, he put on a breastpiece. On the front of it were twelve different stones. These precious gems were not for decoration.

They were a reminder. Each represented one of the twelve

tribes. Every single man, woman, boy, and girl was represented in these stones.

Every time Aaron put on that breastpiece and saw them, God wanted him to remember the people. There wasn't one person in all of Israel God didn't love or care about. And God wanted Aaron to love and care for them as well.

The passage says the stones were to be the means of decision making. In other words, as Aaron faced ministry decisions, he was to ask, "What's best for the people?"

I wonder how often we ever take the time to stop and ask, "What's best for our people?" If the people I lead are really "on my heart," it can't help but impact how I make decisions. I've heard Rick Warren say tongue in cheek, "Many pastors love crowds, they just don't like people." There is more truth in his statement than we want to admit.

Ultimately, leadership is not just about vision and strategy, it's about people. This seems so obvious and yet can be difficult to keep in focus. In the name of vision we can steamroll over others. However, we can't forget that it wasn't vision or a mission statement that was on the breastpiece—it was a symbol of people.

I wonder if God built this reminder into Aaron's ministry because he knows how easy it is to lose sight of people. And, really loving people is demanding work. It's much easier to sit at my computer or plan an event. Really loving on people and investing in them is messy and time-consuming, but there's no substitute for personal care.

I recently talked with a large-church pastor who was concerned his staff was losing their passion for people. He feared they were spending more and more time in front of a computer screen and less and less time in front of a person.

I'm sure Aaron struggled with this too. I'm sure there were days he showed up, put on his breastpiece, and carried out his assignment, but his heart was far from the people. I am sure there were days he went through the motions. There have been lots of days I wanted to hide out in my office and not have to deal with anybody. I've experienced plenty of times when the people weren't on my heart, but they were on my nerves!

I know that to be a faithful pastor I have to love people. The challenge is trying to stay healthy enough so that I can *really* love people.

It really is my desire to have the same feelings Paul had toward those he ministered to in Philippi: "It is right that I should feel as I do about all of you, for you have a very special place in my heart."[2]

"You have a very special place in my heart." Let those words sink in. Would the people I lead say they're on my heart? Would the people in your ministry say they have a very special place in yours? Too many of us have the head of a leader but not the heart of a shepherd.

When life and ministry move too fast, one of the casualties is the personal care and attention of those on our team. Without being aware of it, our mindset toward people can slowly begin to change. Even though all vision is ultimately about touching and impacting *people*, we can do it in a way that's very impersonal. Think how ironic it would be to have a vision about people that ultimately devalues them.

Leadership that is Christ-honoring is never accomplished at the expense of those under our leadership. Here are some practical ways to keep your heart soft toward people.

Stay relationally connected. If you're not authentically experiencing biblical community and personally enjoying life-giving relationships, your own heart will become hard toward others.

Stay spiritually connected to Christ. Ministry is draining and can suck you dry. When you're empty and have nothing to give, you will become impatient, and people will become a nuisance. But when your own soul is healthy and filled up with Christ, your heart will be softer toward others.

Slow down. Try walking slower. When you have a conversation, take time to listen. Hurry is the archenemy of intimacy and deep relationship; it says to people, "I don't really have time for you."

Engage people at a personal level. When was the last time you sat down with somebody on your team and asked, "How are you doing, really?" Maybe take someone in your ministry to lunch with no other agenda than getting to know them.

Just like Aaron would carry his people before the Lord, I want to challenge you to do the same. One of the quickest ways to soften your heart toward others is to pray for them. Would you consider praying by name for a person or two God has called you to serve? I know how easy it is for this to fall off our radar; maybe you could spend a few minutes praying right now before you go back to your day.

May the people you lead always be on your heart.

Questions for Discussion and Reflection

1. Paul said, "It is right that I should feel as I do about all of you, for you have a very special place in my heart." What can you do to help keep the people in your ministry on your heart?

2. If you had a spiritual EKG, would it find you growing softer or harder toward others? Explain.

3. Is there anything you're doing in your ministry that's impersonal or devaluing toward people?

4. Which of the "practical ways to keep your heart soft toward people" listed in this chapter do you need to pay attention to in your ministry?

thirty-one

PAYING ATTENTION

A ttention is one of the most powerful forces in the world. Paying attention is a sign of spiritual health. When you give someone your attention, you are saying, "You matter," "I am interested in you," and "I've got time for you."

Psychologists use the word *attunement* to describe a phenomenon that happens with babies. A baby in a crib, at some moment, looks up and notices a face looking back. Someone is paying attention. For the first time, the baby realizes he or she is connected to—in tune with—another person. When the baby smiles, the other face smiles back.

Attention is an incredible gift; once we discover it, we realize we can't live without it.

A popular Old Testament blessing says, "The Lord bless you and keep you; the Lord make his face shine upon you and be gracious; the Lord turn his face toward you and give you peace."[1]

To turn your face toward someone is to give that person your complete, undivided, interested attention.

Think about that. The eternal and limitless God pays attention to you. He notices you individually. He turns his gracious face toward you. What this blessing describes, Jesus models in the flesh.

Many of the stories from the Gospels are not about Jesus' encounters with the crowds. They are about him paying attention to an individual—Zacchaeus, Bartimaeus, Lazarus, Mary, Martha, the Gerasene demoniac.

One woman Jesus paid attention to is never named. On a very ordinary day, she has an extraordinary encounter. She leaves her house like she has hundreds of times, headed for weekly worship at her local synagogue. She arrives a bit early because she likes to sit in the back; she has a disability that makes navigating crowded areas very difficult.

She's so crippled that for the last eighteen years she hasn't been able to stand up straight. Most people would just stay home. But not this woman. Attending the synagogue was part of her weekly routine and a meaningful act of worship.

On this day, a guest rabbi is teaching. As best as she can, she watches and listens to his message. We're not sure exactly at what point in the message it happens, but the Bible records three powerful words: "Jesus saw her."[2]

He noticed her. She caught his attention. His eyes locked with hers. And he was moved with compassion.

Jesus had a knack for noticing people everyone else seemed to ignore. She would walk out of the synagogue service that day healed and standing straight. And it all happened because Jesus noticed her.

All kinds of people are just waiting to be noticed, to have someone pay attention to them. Every day we pass people who stand up straight, shake your hand, smile, and make small talk, but deep down they're crippled. They almost always try to hide it, but inside they are emotionally bent over. They put up walls, but in their loneliness and quiet desperation, they long to be noticed, to be loved.

As people who are representatives of God himself, one of our specialties ought to be paying attention. For almost every pastor and church leader I know, that really is their heartbeat. They do care. They know they need to pay attention to paying attention.

At least in my life, two very common attention busters come up again and again.

1. *Speed.* You must slow down to notice people. Have you ever noticed that you can't pay attention in a hurry? When you're moving fast, you miss the details. Think of it this way. If someone was standing on the side of the road, would you notice more about them if you flew by them driving seventy-five, or if you walked by them on the sidewalk? The speed of our lives causes us to miss many people God wants us to notice.

Here are tactical ideas that can help you practice what I know is in your heart.

- Look people in the eye. Just like that baby in the crib, there is something about a face paying attention to us that connects us and communicates significance.
- Ask questions. Another way to slow your internal motor is to really engage conversation with good questions. Questions communicate care and interest. Rather than trying to move the conversation along so you can get to your next task, engage and enjoy.
- Leave margin in your daily routine. When every single moment is spoken for, you leave yourself no time for the divine interruptions God wants to send your way. Most of Jesus' life-changing encounters were unplanned and unscheduled.

2. *Preoccupation.* Even if I leave room in my routine, I may not have any mental bandwidth to pay attention to people. Paying

attention not only requires me to be physically present, I must be emotionally and mentally present as well.

I honestly don't know three easy steps to eliminate being preoccupied. However, what I've observed in my own life is this: Paying attention to my soul and my life with Jesus results in being less preoccupied with the stresses and pressures of ministry. Having a healthy soul may not change my outward circumstances, but it makes my heart soft toward people in spite of my circumstances.

Preoccupation and speed can derail my ability to pay attention. On the positive side, I am learning a principle that enhances my ability to notice people: *intention precedes attention.*

I must raise my spiritual antenna and actually scout out people God wants me to notice. Think of it like the *Where's Waldo?* books. In the busy, cluttered pages of your life and ministry, God wants you to find some Waldos. And you'll only see them if you're on the lookout. This week, be like God and turn your face toward people.

Questions for Discussion and Reflection

1. In your past, who paid attention to you who had a significant impact on your life?

2. What are some practical ways you could raise the "paying attention" quotient in your life and ministry?

3. What keeps you from really paying attention to people?

4. Which of the bullet points listed in this chapter could be most helpful to you in paying attention to people?

thirty-two

SHOCK ABSORBERS FOR THE SOUL

He will not fight or shout or raise his voice in public. He will not crush the weakest reed or put out a flickering candle. Finally he will cause justice to be victorious.[1]

These cryptic words were recorded by Isaiah and described Jesus, the coming Messiah. They speak volumes about his ministry. They don't really address the "what" of his ministry, but they do speak of the "how."

Jesus did not come to cajole or manipulate people like some kind of religious charlatan. He did not come to debate or lead by forceful personality. He never tried to gather a crowd or build an organization.

Rather, Isaiah portrays a gentle, compassionate, tender-toward-people Messiah. In ancient times reeds were sometimes used to make a musical instrument. But when the reed became soft or cracked, it became worthless and was tossed aside. And when a lamp burned all the way down to the wick, it would smolder and not produce any light.

Like a cracked reed or a smoldering wick, broken people are often cast aside. Thank God that Jesus doesn't love us or value us based on our usefulness or potential. Of all the possible descriptions Isaiah could have used to portray the style of Jesus' ministry, I am intrigued that he singled out the qualities of humility and gentleness.

Gentleness seems counterintuitive in our take-charge, Type-A, hard-driving leadership model.

A hard-driving leader himself, Bill Hybels observes,

> It stands to reason, then, that a leader sometimes seems to be three-fourths steamroller and one-fourth caring and compassionate colleague. When a leader walks into a meeting, for example, he or she usually has only one thing on the brain: mission advancement.[2]

I wonder how many times over the last thirty years I have been more organizational steamroller than relational people-builder.

When's the last time you heard a conference session or a podcast on the topic of gentleness? When's the last time you heard a fellow leader pray for a more gentle spirit? We pray for vision, impact, and influence. We speak "Prayer of Jabez" kinds of prayers.

Yet the New Testament elevates gentleness more than leadership. For example:

- Jesus says he is gentle and humble in heart.[3]
- Paul says an overseer should be gentle.[4]
- Paul told Timothy to pursue gentleness.[5]
- Paul says he and his fellow workers treated new believers with gentleness, like a mother caring for her children.[6]

Another appropriate translation for "gentleness" would be *graciousness*. I believe this is one of the most endearing qualities a leader can possess. A healthy leader is gracious. A godly leader is gracious. I've learned that a person's ability to communicate on the platform doesn't tell me much about their godliness, but a person's graciousness off the platform tells me a great deal about their humility and Christlikeness.

When I think of gentleness and graciousness, Olav is the poster child. Olav is an older pastor from Norway. One time when he was attending a conference at Saddleback, I invited him to dinner at our home. Even though he was well into his seventies, I knew he would connect with my kids, who were in their early twenties, and I wanted them to be exposed to one of the most gracious men I have ever been around.

When I greeted Olav at the door, he stretched out his arms and in Hebrew gave a blessing over our home and family. For the next three hours I watched him delight in us and in the Lord. I don't remember much about the conversation that night, but I do remember how kind and tender and gracious he was with each person in our family. Olav is that rare person who doesn't make you want to be like him; he makes you want to be like Jesus. I am convinced that one major reason he has such impact is his masterful gentleness.

Gentleness is sort of like holding a newborn baby. An infant is vulnerable, fragile, and easily hurt. So we carefully take them into our hands. We hold them delicately yet securely. We're cautious because we would never want to damage such a precious treasure.

This is how we should treat others. No matter what exterior they project, they are fragile, delicate, and easily hurt.

If tenderness, care, and kindness are the attributes of gentleness, then intimidation, domination, and manipulation are its antithesis. When we "power up," we lose our gentleness. When we are self-serving, we lose our gentleness.

As pastors and ministry leaders, we love to quote Philippians 4. Paul tells us to

- Rejoice in the Lord always.
- Not be anxious about anything.
- Present our requests to God.
- Think on that which is noble and true.

Tucked right in the middle of that passage is a verse that doesn't get the same airtime: "Let your gentleness be evident to all. The Lord is near."[7]

I am intrigued by the four-word addendum to Paul's exhortation to gentleness: "The Lord is near." He could be saying God is near, and he will help you. Treating people with gentleness isn't always easy, and I need God's power to be gentle.

Or, it's possible Paul's saying God is near and watching. How I treat people does not go unnoticed. God isn't just interested in my ministry to the masses—he also cares deeply about my treatment of individuals.

In my own life and in the life of other leaders, I have observed that when I'm emotionally empty and spiritually unhealthy, I am not gentle.

Emotional vitality and spiritual health are like having a good set of shock absorbers for your soul. When shocks are working right, they help absorb life's bumps and potholes. But when your shocks are worn out and you hit a pothole, you bottom out and the ride is rough.

I also need to remember that when my soul isn't healthy, I make the ride rough for everybody else in the car. I regularly see people who are gifted and skilled on the platform. They inspire and they lead. But off the platform they are demanding, angry, impatient, and insensitive. The verbal shrapnel coming from them is anything but gentle.

It should be true that the longer we know and serve Jesus, we grow in graciousness, not grumpiness.

A question for leaders to ask is, "Do those who know me best respect me most?" I'm not talking about respect for you as a visionary or an organizational leader. Do those who have a front-row seat to my life see a leader who's personal, tender, gracious, and gentle?

"Let your gentleness be evident to all."

Questions for Discussion and Reflection

1. Who do you know that has a gentle spirit? What do they do that conveys gentleness?

2. What would it look like for your ministry or church to be more gentle?

3. What are gentleness busters in your life? When are you least likely to be gentle?

4. How are the people in your world impacted when you lack gentleness?

thirty-three

THE BLESSING OF VOICE AND THE VOICE OF BLESSING

As the old axiom says, "Words create worlds." As a leader, your words have power. People pay attention to what you say (or don't say). Our words have staying power in the lives of those we lead.

Part of creating a healthy team environment is learning to bless people with our words. In a world where people are verbally battered, we have the privilege of being the voice of blessing. It's not only a privilege, it's also a sacred trust.

As Proverbs says, life and death are in the tongue.[1] Mother Teresa once said, "Kind words can be short and easy to speak but their echoes are truly endless." Your words, both helpful and hurtful, reverberate through the lives of the people around you.

The ROI on this is huge. For very little investment, there is amazing return. It takes very little time or effort to bless people with our words, but the impact can be profound.

As we talked about earlier, one day while Jesus is teaching, he sees a woman crippled many years; she can't stand up straight. He calls her forward, lays hands on her, heals her on the spot. It's a real, live, verifiable miracle, and everybody there knows it.

But the leader of the synagogue is incensed because Jesus has healed on the Sabbath. He absurdly says, "What you've done violates our policies. You can't heal people today." People like this have an uncanny timing for absolutely wrecking a God moment. I love that Jesus never put human policy over people.

Jesus doesn't back down. He defends his actions and refers to the woman he just healed. But this time he doesn't just call her "woman." He calls her a "daughter of Abraham." He doesn't see her as an old crippled lady. He sees her as a child of the great patriarch of the Jewish people.[2]

I've often tried to imagine her walking home that day, standing up straight for the first time in almost twenty years. She's looking people in the eye, and she's noticing the trees and buildings in her town. She feels ten feet tall. She is seeing things she hasn't seen in years. And ringing in her ears are the words "daughter of Abraham, daughter of Abraham."

Wow. She not only got healed on the outside that day, but I suspect some inner healing took place as well. The Messiah had not seen her as an invalid or a cripple, but as *a daughter of Abraham,* someone who mattered.

I still carry in my notebook a letter I received some time back. It was from someone I've never met—the mom of a pastor on my team. In three or four paragraphs, she shared with me the impact my life and leadership had on her son. Every so often when I'm looking for something, I'll run across that letter. Several times I've pulled it out and read it again. I have taken a lot of life from the words of a lady to whom I've never spoken.

Paul commands us to "encourage one another and build each other up."[3] Many of the messages people hear from the world aren't messages that build them up. They hear, "You're not young enough, you're not smart enough, you're not thin enough, you're not fast enough, you're not *good* enough." It reminds me of Norm, the great theologian on *Cheers*. One day as he came into the bar he said, "It's a dog-eat-dog world, and I'm wearing Milk-Bone underwear."

In a world where people are chewed up and put down, we have the unbelievable privilege of saying, "You matter, your life counts, God loves you, and I am glad you're in my life." Your words may be the only encouraging ones some people hear. You are the voice of God's grace to those around you.

Being an encourager requires you to shift from looking down and in to looking up and out. If we will just notice, if we will just pay attention, the need and opportunity for encouragement is everywhere. People in your ministry, people in your church, and people in your neighborhood are all just waiting to be blessed.

I have a friend with special needs in Calgary named Tyler. He helps out at church by distributing the mail to the staff, and after he's done, you'll find him sitting at a desk with a notebook and pen in hand. Every single day Tyler writes a dozen or so personal notes of encouragement. As his dad once told me, this is Tyler's way of saying, "You were on my mind today."

Here is one of the notes I received from Tyler:

> *Good afternoon lance and connie !*
> *When are you coming back to calgary to visit the staff at centre street church pastor lance ? what are you doing for valentine's next week lance ? i like you buddy lance . from, tyler*

We could all stand to be a little more like Tyler. Life-giving words flow freely from him.

So, how about it? What if we got a little radical and creative with life-giving words? What would it look like for you to be excessive, obnoxious, and over the top with your encouragement this week? Singlehandedly, you can lift someone's spirits, change the atmosphere in your office, or lighten the burden of someone in your small group.

This reminds me of a moment after the Resurrection, the final time Jesus would be with the disciples before ascending. And, guess what he is doing?

> While he was *blessing* them, he left them and was taken up into heaven.[4]

The very last thing Jesus does on earth before returning to the Father is speak words of blessing and encouragement.

May your conversations this week be peppered with phrases like "I believe in you," "I'm grateful for you," "I see God using you," "I appreciate you," and "I'm glad you are in my life."

Remember the admonition of Solomon: Words can kill and words can give life. The choice is yours.

Questions for Discussion and Reflection

1. Describe a time when someone meaningfully impacted you with their words.

2. How prominent is encouragement within your ministry? In what ways do you best hand out encouragement and affirmation?

3. What would it look like for you to be excessive, obnoxious, and over the top with your encouragement this week?

4. Who comes to mind right now that needs encouragement? What step will you take this week to build them up?

thirty-four

THE GIFT OF LOITERING

I just spent a couple days with two really good friends. The setting was perfect—a beautiful house in the mountains, fresh snow, a blazing fire, good food, and plenty of hot coffee. They left about an hour ago, and I'm staying behind for a couple of days to write and be with God.

The house is now empty, but my soul is full. Over the last forty-eight hours we laughed, reminisced, confessed, bantered, evaluated, dreamed, reflected, and planned. There was no posturing or pretense . . . we know each other way too well to play those games. The conversations were honest, rich, personal, and stimulating.

And, I find myself wanting to loiter . . . to linger over the gift of these last two days. I want to *stop* long enough to let my soul soak and marinate in what just happened. I have this profound sense that the afterglow of such an experience provides a wonderful platform for God to speak to me. My heart is soft and my spirit is open. Like taking in a spectacular sunset, I want to stay in the moment.

In fact, I don't think it's a stretch to say that "lingering" is the completion of the experience; lingering is usually followed by awe and gratitude. Maybe the reason there isn't much awe and gratitude in the lives of Christians is that there isn't much lingering.

I want more *slow and deep* in my life, and less *fast and shallow*. Lingering is one practice that helps me. Lingering helps me to slow down, to savor, to deeply experience. Honestly, I'm not very good at this. My default mode is to quickly move back into the world of productivity . . . tasks, projects, and lists.

When I was a kid, I was asked to go on vacation with the Maxwell family. They had five kids and a big clunky green station wagon. I quickly learned they didn't vacation travel like my family. The few times our family went on vacation, we were all about the destination. Our goal was to reach our target destination as quickly as possible, with as few stops as possible, and with as few fights as possible. There was to be no fun or relaxation until we arrived. And it was imperative that your bladder hit full when the gas tank hit empty.

Well, the Maxwells had a totally different philosophy of vacationing. My first clue was that we didn't pull out of the driveway at the appointed time. They'd obviously not been to vacation boot camp; they didn't even synchronize their watches! Even more bizarre was that they weren't stressed out about it. They just didn't seem to be in a hurry at all.

We finally pulled out of the driveway and headed out of town. After about thirty minutes on the road, I noticed Mr. Maxwell slowing down and pulling off the highway. I was pretty sure we didn't have a flat; there was no noticeable mechanical problem; no one was fighting. I couldn't imagine why we were stopping.

As we were all piling out of the car, I asked what was going on. I was informed we had stopped so we could all read the Historical Marker sign. I thought they were kidding. They were not. We would be stopping at all the historical markers along the trip.

Our family had never stopped once at a historical marker. We scoffed at people who did. Didn't the Maxwells know life is too short to waste time reading signs? Didn't they know it's about the destination, not the journey?

The Maxwells knew, and I'm just now learning, that lingering is a good thing. Taking time to enjoy a dusty old historical marker actually added to the experience; it didn't diminish it. *They also believed that the vacation began when you start, not when you arrive.* When that's your mindset, it's okay to enjoy moments along the way.

The Bible frequently calls on us to linger. The challenge to "remember" or "think" or "meditate" is often an invitation to do so.

- *Think* of the wonderful works he has done, the miracles, and the judgments he handed down.[1]
- I lie awake *thinking* of you, *meditating* on you through the night.[2]
- I *remember* the days of old. I *ponder* all your great works. I *think* about what you have done.[3]
- Every time I *think* of you, I give thanks to my God.[4]

When I *think* of my two friends, I give thanks to my God. So, how about it? Why not put this book down for a few moments and just linger.

What unexpected gift did you receive today? Maybe it was a teachable moment with your child or a Bible verse that was just what you needed or encouragement from a good friend or just another day of life.

What about making a commitment to becoming a spiritual loiterer? Instead of rushing on to the next thing you have to do . . . STOP. REFLECT. THINK. PONDER.

Questions for Discussion and Reflection

1. When did you recently take time to loiter (linger) over something beautiful?

2. What small thing brings you great delight and joy?

3. How good are you and your ministry at lingering to celebrate God's good gifts?

4. As you linger over your spiritual journey, what are you most grateful for today?

BUILDING HEALTHY TEAMS

thirty-five

"TEAM" DOESN'T HAVE AN "I," BUT IT DOES HAVE A "YOU"

I am often asked, "How do you know if a church is healthy?" Diagnosing the health of a church is certainly more art than science. But if you were going to hold your spiritual stethoscope to a church and listen for what's going on inside, the place I'd start would be the staff/leadership culture.

I know this for sure: You can't diagnose the health of a ministry by its size or rate of growth. Nor can you diagnose it by what happens on the platform on Sunday mornings.

If you want to talk about an organization's true spiritual health, you have to look at the health of the team that leads it.

The first step to building a healthy staff and leadership culture is to get it on the radar. We get so busy trying to grow the organization that we neglect to grow and develop our team. If your team is your greatest asset, it's not only right to invest in them, it's also strategic to the fulfillment of the vision.

A healthy staff culture does not happen by accident. You

won't drift into it any more than you would drift into a healthy marriage.

Let me also say this loud and clear: You cannot assume your team is spiritually and emotionally healthy just because you are in a church or ministry.

Once it's *on* your radar, how do you start building a healthy team culture?

Personal Care

The people on my team have to know I care about them personally, not just professionally. I must value them for who they are, not just what they can do.

I remember years ago talking to a friend about my marriage. I asked, "What can I do to make my wife feel more valued?" He said, "Well, maybe if you truly start valuing her, she will feel valued." *Ouch.* I was looking for some quick fix, some technique. My friend was wise enough to point me to my own heart.

A lot of leaders want the quick fix in personally caring for their staff. So, we have an annual Christmas party and think we've celebrated and personally cared for our staff. While that party might be a good thing, this isn't the kind of personal care I'm talking about.

I'm talking about the kind of care that regularly conveys, "What matters most is not what we want *from* you, but what we want *for* you. We care about your marriage. We care about your kids. We care about your health. We care about your walk with God."

I'm talking about the kind of personal care that says, "We care about your rhythm of life. We want you to be at your kids' soccer games. We want you to have your day off. We want you to take your vacation time."

In *Relational Intelligence* Steve Saccone says, "Consumers always look for what they can take from others, while investors always look for what they can give to others."[1] Do those we lead feel like they're invested in or like a commodity that's consumed?

Making people feel invested in starts with personal care. It could be as simple as a one-minute hallway conversation that isn't ministry-related. It could be praying for and with someone about something besides a ministry goal. It could be reminding a young staff member to spend time with their kids because they will never get these days back.

For a season at Saddleback I sent a birthday card with a personal note to every staff member. My assistant would hand me a stack of cards each week, and I would spend a half hour writing notes. For those on my team I would also send an anniversary card because I wanted them to know I cared about their marriages. On their kids' birthdays I would send a card with a five-dollar coupon for yogurt. You can invest in personal care for very little time and almost no expense.

Sense of Family

In order for your team to be healthy, there must be a sense of family. You must learn to laugh together, cry together, and resolve conflict together.

In a church I pastored, I decided to get intentional about building community within our team, and it seemed the best place to start was our weekly meetings. At the time our staff was fifteen or twenty people. We took the first thirty minutes to deepen our relationships and build a greater sense of family.

This was not easy for me. I like "productive" meetings where we make decisions and come up with action plans. I like a clear agenda and clear outcomes. For Type-A leaders, "building family" can seem way too touchy-feely.

I also knew that if we didn't put this in the first part of the meeting, we'd never get around to it. Each week we would start with a simple question about growing up, about family, about favorite memories, about life-shaping experiences. As I think back, that first half hour is what I remember. We belly-laughed, we empathized, and we cared. Most of all, we really got to know each other . . . and we became family.

Another critical component for building family is people telling their story. This can be time-consuming, but the payoff is huge, and there are several benefits to the team.

Storytelling gives insight that explains why this person is like they are. It helps the team know better how to work with him or her. It helps the team care about more than just what they contribute to the organization. And it will strengthen relational bonds.

You might want to consider having a different team member share their story each week. Give them advance notice and set aside a half hour to an hour for them to share and for the group to interact with their story.

A few questions that will help prime the pump as people prepare to share their story:

- What have been some turning points/defining moments in your life?
- What experiences (good and bad) have shaped you?
- Who had the most significant influence on your life? How did they influence you?
- When have you felt successful? When have you felt God's pleasure?
- What was life like growing up? Describe your home life.
- Describe the most difficult season of your spiritual journey.`
- What has been the biggest transition in your life?
- What has been your greatest disappointment?
- What was your view of God growing up?
- In recent years, how has your relationship with God grown and changed?
- How would you want to be remembered?

Why not blow away your team this week? When you have your meeting, take the first thirty minutes and make the people the first agenda item. Have some fun. Get to know each other. Laugh a little. Build family.

Questions for Discussion and Reflection

1. How would you describe the spiritual health of your ministry team?

2. How intentional are you and your team at building a great team culture?

3. How much emphasis is given to the personal care of the team members? What would make your team feel more personally cared for?

4. What steps could you take to build a strong sense of community into your team?

thirty-six

IS YOUR TEAM CULTURE MORE CORPORATE THAN CHRISTLIKE?

A re the people on your team better Christ followers because of your leadership? Are those you lead better Christians because they've been hanging around you and your ministry?

If you're going to have a spiritually healthy team, you must integrate these two qualities into the fabric of team life.

Authentic Spirituality

There must be a vibrant, life-giving God orientation to how we do team. As you read those words, your reaction might be "Well, of course. After all, we're a ministry. It's a given that there should be prayer and time together in the Word and spiritual growth on the team. That's what we're about."

It's the Christian Life 101, but it's a gaping hole in the life of many staff cultures. We mistakenly assume people are on track spiritually; therefore, we can focus all of our collective efforts on the ministry's vision. We spend our meetings talking about plans and goals. Prayer is like the national anthem at a sporting event, a mere formality. The books we give to staff are about leadership; all the training is about ministry skill.

Over time the environment can begin to feel corporate and lacking in spiritual vitality. The kind of spiritual life we talk about on Sunday is not what the team is experiencing through the week. This becomes a breeding ground for cynicism that can poison the entire leadership culture.

That's why we must work hard to raise our team's spiritual temperature. A great starting place: simply have more God conversations. Share what God has been doing in your life or what he's been teaching you. Ask others what he's been doing.

Another way to raise the spiritual temperature is to regularly open God's Word together. Spend a few minutes unpacking a passage with your team. Memorize a passage together.

Pray together. I mean really pray together, about anything and everything. Have planned times *and* spontaneous times of prayer. Make prayer a part of how you do team.

When I was at Saddleback, God used a little boy named Ethan to help our team learn how to pray together. Ethan's dad, Steve, served on my team. Steve was full of life, a good leader, and a lot of fun. One day in our meeting Steve shared that he and his wife, Lisa, were concerned about Ethan's development; they'd taken him for some tests and the preliminary diagnosis was autism. At the time they weren't sure how severe it might be or all of the implications, but simply hearing that your child might be autistic is enough to terrify you as a parent.

As Steve shared, you could tell he and Lisa were reeling, afraid and anxious, trying to process this new discovery. The news had rocked their world and changed their lives forever. During this tender time, the guys did a great job in rallying around him with lots of prayer and personal care.

As Steve and Lisa walked through the testing and discovery process there were some very difficult days. I remember several occasions over the next few months when Steve shared and all of us sat quietly with tears in our eyes. We didn't have magical words to make the pain go away, but we could care, be present, and pray for this precious family.

Developing People

Ministry leaders are usually better quarterbacks than coaches. We like to be out on the field, personally leading the charge, calling the plays and directing the team.

Coaches are about developing people and getting the very best out of them. While quarterbacks make plays, coaches make players.

If we want healthy teams, we must learn the skills of a coach. The greatest multiplication and impact of your ministry will be through the people you develop.

Parachurch ministries often seem more dialed in to this truth than those of us who lead in the church. Years ago a friend who leads a parachurch college ministry taught me a valuable principle: "More time spent with fewer people equals greater impact." That certainly was the strategy of Jesus. He found a handful of followers and for three years poured himself into them.

Your leadership team, your staff are your handful. How are you doing at developing them?

One of the most definitive passages about discipling and developing people is found in 1 Thessalonians:

> You know that we dealt with each of you as a father deals with his own children, encouraging, comforting and urging you to live lives worthy of God, who calls you into his kingdom and glory.[1]

This passage oozes with relationship, and it's a good reminder that our first priority is to build people, not a program. In the earlier verses Paul said he'd been like a mother caring for her children; he and his team had shared not only the gospel with these believers but their very lives.[2] Now Paul likens himself to a father who encourages, comforts, and urges.

So, how do you know when someone, right now, needs to be encouraged? Or comforted? Or urged (challenged)? The only way you know what they need "right now" is to be in relationship with them.

All three actions Paul mentions are crucial in developing people. Encouraging is about affirming and blessing. It is finding people doing something right and praising them. It is helping them discover their unique gifting and contribution.

Comforting is all about helping people through the difficult things. When life gets hard and when ministry gets hard, we walk alongside to provide comfort and support.

Urging is about challenging people—nudging them and pushing them to improve and grow. It is about stretching them and not letting them settle.

Relationship is what gives me the right and insight to encourage, comfort, and urge the people on my team.

Developing people has obvious implications for your schedule. Getting intentional about it may require serious adjustments to how you spend your time. But I can't think of anything with greater long-term benefits than personally developing your team members.

When Paul concludes 1 Thessalonians 2, a chapter largely about developing people, he says, "What is our hope, our joy, or the crown in which we will glory in the presence of our Lord Jesus when he comes? Is it not you? Indeed, you are our glory and joy."[3]

Paul says when Jesus returns the one thing he will be most excited to show him will be these Christians. At the end of the day, what's most important is not the buildings or programs we build but rather the people we develop.

Questions for Discussion and Reflection

1. What do you do with your team to nurture personal spiritual growth?

2. What are some things you could build right into your meetings that would help create a spiritually vibrant team?

3. Who played a development role in your life? What did they do with you that was developmental?

4. Instead of being a better "player," how could you be a better coach for your team?

SPEAK THE
UNSPOKEN RULES

While at Saddleback I had the privilege of leading a great team of pastors. They were all high-capacity, high-octane leaders. And it's a good thing they were, because the environment was high-change and fast-paced. Add to this mix a senior pastor who was an entrepreneurial idea-machine, and you have all the makings of a potentially dysfunctional team environment.

Again, creating a healthy team environment is more art than science, and we weren't the poster children for team health. But one of the steps we took that proved helpful was the creation of a team covenant—a set of operating principles we came up with together and agreed to live by.

What creates dysfunction in a team is what creates dysfunction in any relationship: colliding expectations. With different personalities, backgrounds, and experiences we all show up with our own picture of what "team" means and how a team should function.

This is further complicated by the fact that most organizations and churches do not articulate expectations regarding "how we do team around here."

In *Church Unique*, Will Mancini observes,

> Collaboration is lost to sideways energy every day in the local church. Why? The three reasons I see most are mistrust, personal ego, and lack of strategic clarity. . . . Leaders rarely clarify what working together really looks like.[1]

Imagine you're driving down the road and start encountering a bit of fog. This causes you to focus and really pay attention, but you can still see what's up ahead. That's how I would describe a lot of churches and ministries when it comes to their vision and values. It may not be crystal clear, but there is some sense of what the church is about.

As you drive on the fog becomes thicker. You're forced to slow down; navigating becomes more difficult. You're tense and uptight as you try to stay on the road.

This thicker fog is a good picture of the staff and team culture of many churches. It's even more unclear and unarticulated than the church's missional objectives.

It's very possible to have organizational clarity and team chaos. And you can have functional plans but dysfunctional teams. The result is a lot of tension and stress as people try to stay out of the ditch. Fog is dangerous when driving and dangerous when trying to build a team.

When I first joined the staff, this was a huge challenge for me. I'd been senior pastor of a medium-sized church; now the staff was bigger than most churches.

I constantly found myself trying to discern the team culture. How do we communicate around here? Where are the landmines? How is conflict dealt with? How do decisions get made? I remember sitting down with several staff members and asking, "What is it that no one has likely told me, that I need to know to succeed here?"

Every organization has a team culture, and even though you

can't see it in the organizational fog, it's real. Someone has said culture is the "unspoken rules of how things get done." For team health, it is imperative that someone *speak the unspoken rules*. The team culture of most churches I've been around is squishy, loaded with landmines.

That's why leaders must take responsibility to bring clarity to the team culture. Marcus Buckingham, who writes about maximizing strengths, says, "Clarity is the preoccupation of the effective leader. If you do nothing else as a leader, be clear."[2]

As I reflect back over years of ministry, clarity has not always been a strength for me. What usually got in the way were my own insecurities and people-pleasing tendencies. Trying to be diplomatic and never too rigid, I regularly contributed to the fog.

In an effort to bring clarity to our dynamics, we decided to develop a team covenant. Our team covenant wasn't something I came up with and then handed out to the team. It was a collaborative exercise. If the team is going to "stack hands" and really live by these, they need to have significant input. Also, group participation allows people to articulate the values and expectations important to them in "doing team."

The exercise itself turned out to be a great team-building experience. It was encouraging to see these hard-driving leaders desire spiritual growth and personal care as part of our team dynamic.

You will notice, in the covenant we came up with, that some of the statements are very general and others very specific. Some talk about how we would operate professionally; some focus on how we would care for each other personally.

One of the benefits that came from the covenant is that it gave clear boundaries. When those got violated, it was easier to have the hard conversation, for two reasons. First, we had mutually developed the tenets and had all agreed to abide by them. Second, they were written down. There was no fog.

Because Saddleback was an e-mail-driven culture, one of

the most common violations was doing e-mail during meetings. Offenders got busted not just by me but by the whole group.

If you want a high-performance, spiritually healthy team, the fog must begin to lift, and a team covenant will help.

TEAM COVENANT

- *We will openly voice and express our own opinions and it is safe to voice contrary opinions.*
- *We will follow through with our commitments.*
- *We will agree to support and invest in each other personally and professionally.*
- *We will pray for each other and with each other.*
- *We will hold and respect all confidences.*
- *We will have frank and open discussion within the room, solidarity outside the room.*
- *We will strive to help each other win.*
- *Silence is agreement.*
- *We will have fun.*
- *Show up on time.*
- *No e-mail during meetings (except during breaks).*
- *Communicate often and constantly ask "who needs to know."*
- *We will not verbally "throw each other under the bus" when we speak of one another.*

Questions for Discussion and Reflection

1. Would you describe your team culture as more foggy, or more clear? Why?

2. What is most unclear about your team culture?

3. What's the one thing about your ministry culture that every staff member must know in order to succeed?

4. If you were drafting a team covenant, what would you personally want included? Share at least two items.

thirty-eight

SHOW UP AND
SPEAK UP

D ishonesty creates dysfunction, and terminal niceness can be terminal to the health of a ministry.
Most of us who lead are just not very good at hard
conversations. Usually we are polite, we are sensitive, and we hate
conflict. We beat around the bush, tap dance around the conflict,
and make nice.

A huge part of team health has to do with how well we interact and communicate. It takes courage and consistency to create a
culture of open, honest, candid communication.

In *Fierce Conversations*, Susan Scott says,

> Our lives succeed or fail gradually, then suddenly, one
> conversation at a time. While no single conversation is guar-
> anteed to change the trajectory of a career, a business, a mar-
> riage, or a life, any single conversation can. The conversation
> is the relationship.[1]

Let those words soak in: "The conversation is the relationship."

Unless we learn how to have more honest conversations, we will have shallow relationships. Unless we learn to talk about the hard and uncomfortable stuff, our sense of authentic community will be purely cosmetic.

To the casual onlooker, it can seem like a team gets along well and has healthy relationships; they see people being polite, kind, civil, and respectful. But private hallway conversations reveal a different reality. The conflict, tension, and strong opinions that are not welcome in the team meeting are welcome in the hallway. Everyone quickly figures out that in the team meeting you make nice and play it safe. And, unfortunately, teams who don't engage conflict "resort to veiled discussions and guarded comments."[2]

At the first hint of conflict in a team meeting, many people will turtle up. When you pick up a turtle, what does it do? Sticks his head into his protective shell. The more you prod and poke, and beat on the shell, the deeper he withdraws. It's a defense mechanism. The turtle will not stick his head out again until he feels it's safe to do so. The same is true for people.

As a leader, *I must begin to create a safe environment, infused with trust, where we talk about the hard stuff and engage conflict in a healthy way.* When people take the risk of sticking their neck out and disagreeing, we must not shut them down. Nothing will cause turtling up quicker than use of power, position, guilt, or defensiveness; in contrast, we want to foster openness and bless honest feedback.

A friend of mine was in a team meeting where there was palpable conflict. As he described the leader's reaction, he likened him to "the big bully on the playground," through intimidation quickly shutting down the conversation. Everyone in the room turtled up. I guarantee it will be a long time before they venture out of their shell again.

So, from a leader's standpoint, we must create a culture and environment that fosters openness and blesses honest feedback.

From a team member's standpoint, *once I sense there is a safe environment, I have the responsibility to show up and speak up.* I must engage and not hold back. The team needs my input. I see things others don't. My perspective and experience are unique.

Take a few moments for self-assessment by reflecting on the following.

- How many times have I held back in a meeting because I was afraid of what others would think?
- How often have I found myself saying things I don't really believe just to be polite?
- How often have I seen something that isn't right but didn't say anything because I didn't want to cause trouble?
- How often have I seen someone about to make a bad decision and said nothing?
- How many times have I sat silent while the big elephant in the room is ignored?
- How many times have I participated in gossip about a team member rather than having the hard, honest conversation with him or her?
- How many times have I tolerated inappropriate and hurtful behavior because I wasn't willing to have the hard conversation?

These are hard and painful questions for me. I have spent enormous time and energy over the years making nice. Some of the biggest conflict and pain I have experienced in ministry (and caused others to experience) might have been avoided if I just would have shown up and spoken up.

Years ago a conflict came up with someone on my team. I had growing concern about his decisions, attitude, and style of leadership. Priding my diplomatic skills, I thought I could correct these issues without creating a big ordeal. I was wrong.

Over a couple of years, the situation continued to deteriorate until finally the decision was made to let him go. It was painful and messy. A few weeks later, his counselor, following up so that we could learn from this experience, told us, "Part of the problem was that you weren't clear in your communication, and the byproduct was that he never really heard you." My unwillingness to confront the issues candidly ended up creating much confusion and hurt. Even if I'd been more forthright, I am not sure things could have been rescued, but he and his family deserved better communication.

Once more, Solomon said, "An honest answer is like a kiss of friendship."[3] Holding back or turtling up is not a kiss of friendship; it's an honest answer that says, "I value you enough to tell you what I really think," and "I care about you too much to be silent." When I don't show up and speak up, it is usually because I am thinking of me. I want my comments and non-comments to put me in the best light. But if I really care about the team and the relationships, I will be honest. I'll give my feedback and share my concerns.

There's a definite irony here. Trying not to upset people and make waves makes just the opposite happen. In our attempt to avoid conflict, we actually end up creating it.

Questions for Discussion and Reflection

1. When it comes to having hard, honest conversations, what has been your pattern?

2. How open, honest, and candid is the culture of communication in your ministry or church?

3. How well do you think your team does in confronting and resolving conflict?

4. What proactive steps can you take to create a safe environment where people feel free to show up and speak up?

thirty-nine

ARE YOUR SYSTEMS VITAMINS OR TOXINS?

J ust beneath your skin is a set of complex systems that make your body work. These ten systems (nervous, respiratory, reproductive, etc.) are vital to your health and existence. If you neglect them, over time they will degenerate and become diseased. On the flip side, if you pay attention to your body's systems, you can extend your life's length and quality.

What is true of the body is also true of churches and ministries. Making your ministry function are basic systems like communication, lines of authority, budget, calendaring, programming, hiring, and decision making. The long-term health of your church/ ministry is absolutely driven by and dependent on the health of these systems.

You can have a great platform ministry with a great communicator and great worship music, but if the systems underneath are diseased and broken, the health of the ministry will eventually deteriorate.

Most every ministry leader I know has the desire and good

intention to have a spiritually healthy team. But you can no more wish spiritual health into existence than you can wish physical health into existence. It takes more than an occasional staff devotional or team prayer meeting to create a healthy team. It will take more than a catchy vision statement. As Andy Stanley says, "The system down the hall trumps the mission on the wall." It takes intentional systems that foster health.

Systems modify behavior, which in turn creates healthy habits that result in positive change.

So let me challenge you. Think about the systems inside your church or ministry. Are they contributing to health, or are they perpetuating dysfunction? Are your values reflected in the way these systems function? What might have to change for your systems to get healthier?

These are questions worth serious reflection and conversation.

Let's take a look at a clear biblical example of a broken system.

In Exodus 18 the people of Israel were headed to the Promised Land. Moses had been separated from his wife and boys, so his father-in-law, Jethro, had brought them home. The following day Jethro went to work with Moses.

Moses took his seat and from morning until evening settled disputes and served as the only judge for more than two million people. Think of all the wasted time spent waiting in line to get a few minutes with Moses. It was worse than the DMV office.

Any dispute that could not be settled was brought to him, no matter how small or big. When Jethro watched this for a day, he said, "What is this you are doing for the people? Why do you alone sit as judge, while all these people stand around you from morning till evening?" That's a nice way of saying, "Have you lost your mind?"

Listen to Moses' response: "Because the people come to me to seek God's will." What was painfully obvious to Jethro wasn't obvious to Moses at all. It's like he says, "That's just how we roll here. There are a lot of needs, and people come to me looking for help. I just stay at it and work until everyone gets an answer." Sometimes we are so accustomed to doing things one way that we can't see how broken the system really is.

Jethro responded, "What you are doing is not good. You and these people who come to you will only wear yourselves out." Moses was the bottleneck of a system that was broken and creating dysfunction, wasting time and energy and wearing everyone out.

When we have poorly devised and poorly functioning systems, we will wear out ourselves and our team. You'll end up spending a lot of sideways energy managing the problems of a broken system. At times it might be wise to consult an outsider like Jethro who can see things more clearly and objectively.

The system Jethro proposed was three-pronged: Pray. Teach. Delegate. Moses was to *pray* and take the people's needs before God. He was to *teach* the people so they would know God's laws and be able to settle most disputes themselves. And, he was to find faithful men and *appoint* them as officials over thousands, hundred, fifties, and tens.

Notice that the healthy system would allow Moses time to pray. When a culture is dominated by ineffective and dysfunctional systems, spiritual practices get marginalized. Healthy systems actually create space and time for spiritual life.

Jethro offers the hope of a preferred future, a future culture with healthy systems: "If you do this and God so commands, you will be able to stand the strain, and all these people will go home satisfied."[1] When good systems are in place, leaders stay in the game longer and the people we serve "go home satisfied."

To stimulate your thinking, let me offer some what-if possibilities for your systems.

Hiring. What if you . . .

- really took the time to hear and understand a candidate's life journey

- explored not just leadership competencies, but spiritual health as well
- gathered the very best possible interview questions
- did personality and strength testing to insure a good fit
- were able to offer a crystal clear job description to a potential candidate
- were totally honest about the good, the bad, and the ugly rather than giving the candidate a recruiting speech
- were to partner them with someone who would help them assimilate into the family and culture of your team

Work and family balance. What if you . . .
- communicated that staff are expected to take their days off
- told your team that you wanted them to practice Sabbath
- offered counseling to families in need
- communicated a maximum number of hours you want your staff to work in a week
- told your staff you didn't want them responding to e-mails when they are supposed to be with their family

Team dynamic. What if you . . .
- helped every team develop a covenant
- taught listening skills to the team
- started creating a culture of honest but respectful interaction
- developed guidelines for the appropriate use of technology
- trained every team in how to build community/family into their team life
- began training your people in conflict resolution skills

Spiritual formation. What if you . . .
- integrated prayer and fasting into your ministry rhythm

- started reading books together about matters of the soul instead of just leadership
- implemented personal retreats as a way to help keep your team members spiritually replenished
- got into the habit of asking questions like "What's God been teaching you lately?" or "How is it with your soul?"

This is not a quick fix. Just like it took Moses time to build and implement a new system, it will take us time as well. But if we can do this well, just maybe we won't wear out ourselves or our team.

Questions for Discussion and Reflection

1. Overall, what is your opinion of the systems within your ministry? Are they helpful? Cumbersome? Adequate? Do they promote team health?

2. What ministry system do you feel best about?

3. What ministry system needs the most attention?

4. If you could implement one systems change to your ministry, what would it be?

forty

GOING BEYOND ALIGNMENT TO ATTUNEMENT

N ot long ago, my car started pulling to the right. I could tell it was out of alignment, but I had no clue how to fix it—I'm what you call mechanically challenged. So I took it to the professionals, who tinkered with the internal structure and systems until everything was aligned. When the car is aligned, it runs more efficiently, creates less wear and tear, and operates more smoothly.

The same is true in creating alignment within our ministries. It takes intentionality; you never drift into alignment. People with skill know how to get down inside the organization and align its systems and structures to increase effectiveness, minimize wasted effort, and achieve greater health.

Alignment is crucial, and there's a lot of talk in organizations today about it. We do want to make sure all our staff and ministries are rowing in the same direction. But while that's a good and needed thing, it's not enough.

There's a huge difference between aligning a car and aligning an organization: It's the difference between parts and people. Aligning a car is a mechanical process; aligning people is relational. Too many leaders approach organizational alignment as a purely mechanical process and underestimate the importance of relationship.

Imagine a magnet on a table with a bunch of iron filings. As you move the magnet around, the filings will begin to move—the force of the magnet's power causes them to fall into place, to be aligned. A magnet creates alignment by strength, power, and force.

But that is not how alignment works in an organization. People do not line up like iron filings. Force and power may create systems alignment, but they will not create heart alignment. That's why a healthy organization must be giving attention not only to alignment but also to attunement.

Attunement has to do with aligning hearts. It's about relationship and bringing people along. It's about creating a sense of ownership and buy-in. I can force alignment organizationally and lead from my positional role, but attunement comes only from relationship, when those who follow us trust us and know we care about them.

This illustration shows the contrast between the focus of alignment and attunement.

Alignment	Attunement
Organizational	Relational
Plans	People
Head	Heart
Ends	Means
Where we're going (goals)	How we get there (team)
Functional outcomes	Emotional buy-in
Cause	Community

As a leader I must learn the art of attunement. It's a soft skill that won't show up on an organizational chart or strategic plan, yet it can make or break an organization's effectiveness. If there is dysfunction and distrust at the people level, it doesn't matter how much you force alignment at the organizational level.

You can't treat people poorly and expect them to lead effectively. Alignment tends to focus on organizational goals, while attunement tends to focus on relational good will.

So, how do you foster attunement that authentically creates emotional buy-in?

Before I share some practical suggestions, let me send up a warning flare. Don't fake it. Don't manipulate or try to create the façade of attunement.

In his great book *It's Your Ship*, Michael Abrashoff says your people

> are more perceptive than you give them credit for, and they always know the score—even when you don't want them to.[1]

Believe in your people. People in our generation carry around a backpack full of insecurities and self-condemnation. When is the last time you looked a team member in the eye and said, "I believe in you; I want to do everything I can to help you succeed"?

Celebrate. Shine a light on what's right. Make heroes out of your team members. "According to the U.S. Department of Labor, the number one reason people leave their jobs is because they do not feel appreciated."[2] "One poll found that an astonishing 65 percent of Americans reported receiving no recognition for good work in the past year."[3] While it's important to publicly recognize team members, don't forget to praise people privately and "in the moment."

Build community. Work hard to build a sense of family among your team. We all love to work with people who have become our friends rather than simply co-workers. In your meetings take time to build relationships. Pray together. Celebrate birthdays. Go to dinner with the team and their spouses. This will pay huge dividends in breaking down silos, creating alignment, and moving the team toward attunement.

Listen aggressively. Listen to people's ideas. Listen to their frustrations. Be accessible and approachable. Give them your undivided, unhurried attention. On the popular reality show *Undercover Boss*, high-powered CEOs go undercover to do the grunge work of their employees and to have conversations at the ground level. It not only has given these CEOs fresh perspective and new respect, but it also has deepened love and personal care for their teams. It has helped with alignment *and* attunement.

Constantly communicate. Communication is a major challenge for most organizations. And as the church or ministry grows, so do the complexities surrounding communication. It really is true that people are "down on" what they're not "up on."

In other words, lack of communication fosters negativity and cynicism. Few things are more demoralizing than being blindsided by a public announcement about something that directly impacts your area. If you want to torpedo attunement, make decisions in isolation rather than collaboration. In a culture of attunement, people feel included, not just informed.

In a fast-paced, ADD, turn-on-a-dime culture like Saddleback, communication was always a struggle. To help my team communicate better, we would regularly try to ask the "who needs to know" question: "Who is going to be impacted by what we talked about today? What are the implications of the decisions we made today?" The decisions that were made reverberated throughout the entire staff.

Have fun. There is nothing unspiritual about fun. Most church staffs I know could stand to raise the fun quotient. We all know our mission is serious and the cause is demanding. But no team can endure intensity and grueling demand all the time. Teams must learn a healthy rhythm that includes a good dose of laughter, fun, and banter. You'll be healthier for it.

I want to ask you to consider taking the attunement challenge. Spend more time this week on attunement than alignment. Focus more on people than plans. Have unhurried conversation with team members that isn't about their leadership, but is about their lives.

Questions for Discussion and Reflection

1. What kind of report card would you give your ministry as far as alignment? Why?

2. What kind of report card would you give as far as attunement? Why?

3. Attunement comes from relationship, which is built on trust. On a scale of 1 (low) to 10 (high), how would you rate the trust level within your ministry? How do you feel about that number?

4. Which one of the italicized suggestions in this chapter could most help bring attunement in your ministry?

forty-one

TEN COMMANDMENTS OF TECHNOLOGY AND TEAM

Virtually anything that can be productive can also be destructive. Whether it's a car, a credit card, a knife, sex, or an iPhone, inappropriate use can do damage.

There's no question this principle applies to technology. Technology has opened unprecedented doors for the gospel. It has given ministries the opportunity to multiply their reach exponentially. It has made biblical knowledge accessible to billions. We live in a "more-faster-now" society.[1] And ministry leaders love it because it means we can dream bigger, do more, and reach further.

But technology also has a dark side.

Technology has created opportunities for sexual predators. It has opened the floodgates to pornography and scam artists. Technology also has numerous subtle and more socially acceptable downsides. It has reduced our attention span, kept us more distracted, and raised the level of white noise in our lives. In his sobering *The Age of Speed*, Vince Poscente writes,

Crackberries have become the unofficial mascot of the Age of Speed, but mind your addiction. Research revealed that allowing frequent email interruptions causes a drop in performance equivalent to losing ten IQ points—two and a half times the drop seen after smoking pot.[2]

Addiction to speed and technology is just as prevalent in the church as in society. Many are choosing to live online rather than in person.

The implications are not limited to the individual; they're also potentially toxic for the team. I have developed "Ten Commandments of Technology and Team" that I believe, if followed, would create a healthier team environment.

1. Thou shalt not use e-mail to deliver bad news.

E-mail is great for relaying information but terrible for confrontation. E-mail works well for disseminating data but is lousy for navigating relationships.

With e-mail there is no chance for the receiver to read your facial expression or body language. Nor can he or she hear your tone. When I'm simply reading an e-mail, I can hear whatever "tone of voice" I want. With e-mail, there is no chance in the moment for response and dialogue. There is no chance in the moment for clarification.

Quite simply, delivering bad news via e-mail is the coward's way out. We dishonor and devalue people when we fire off harsh e-mails like Scud missiles. In a healthy culture, people sit down and have the hard conversations in person.

2. Thou shalt not put anything in e-mail that you would mind having forwarded . . . because it probably will be.

I've learned this lesson the hard way. Several times I've had an e-mail forwarded to people I would not have wanted to receive it. So, when an e-mail deals with anything delicate, I'm learning to ask myself, "Will I mind if this gets forwarded?"

3. Thou shalt not e-mail (or chat online) during meetings.

This was one of the team rules at Saddleback. It's such a temptation to multi-task in a meeting, but the result is we disengage and check out. This is the antithesis of "team."

4. Thou shalt not use "bcc."

Most often, "blind carbon copy" is used to secretly include people in the e-mail without the recipient knowing it. No good thing comes from blind-copying people on your e-mails. While it might have an appropriate use or two, the potential risks and negatives simply don't make it worth using.

At Saddleback, this issue caused some significant pain among the staff. We finally made a decision among the senior leadership that we would not use bcc in our e-mails.

5. Thou shalt be more personal than professional.

By its very nature, e-mail tends to come across as impersonal. Therefore, we have to work hard to come across as warm and personal. Make your e-mails more relational and less transactional. It takes a few extra seconds, but communicate as a friend.

6. Thou shalt keep e-mails short and to the point.

I know there's occasionally a need for a longer e-mail. But, as a general rule, keep it simple and straightforward. With the inundation of information today, people have to filter and sort quickly. Be concise and remove the clutter. In communication, always choose clear over cute.

7. Thou shalt not text or take calls while in conversation or in a meeting.

I am amazed how many conversations I'm in where the other person will respond to a text right in the middle of our interaction. Interrupting a conversation to take a call is devaluing; that's why they invented voicemail. It is the rare occasion when I *must* take a call right this moment. And, if you must take a call while talking to someone else, explain why you need to interrupt the conversation and apologize for having to do so.

8. Thou shalt not call or e-mail people on their day off.

If we're going to create healthy teams, we must begin to work harder at creating margin in people's lives. One way to do so is to honor their time at home with their family and honor their day off or their Sabbath.

We should be proactive to communicate with our team that we want them to live healthy, balanced lives. And, they are not expected to answer e-mails or phone calls when they're off or at home with their family.

9. Thou shalt use e-mail for prayer and encouragement.

Most of these commandments are "thou shalt not," but this one is "thou shalt." E-mail and texting (etc.) are wonderful tools for prayer and encouragement. In a matter of seconds I can send a message that says "you matter; you were on my mind." And I can use e-mail and texting to write out a simple prayer on behalf of someone I care about.

10. Thou shalt give phone/e-mail/Facebook/Twitter (etc.) a Sabbath.

Part of developing a healthy team means developing a healthy rhythm personally. I encourage you to talk with your team about having a technology Sabbath where you literally and symbolically unplug for a day. Imagine what it could be like if for twenty-four hours you had live (instead of virtual) conversations. If you played with your kids instead of your iPhone. If you responded to your spouse instead of your e-mail.

Questions for Discussion and Reflection

1. What is one way technology has negatively impacted your ministry team?

2. How could you use technology to be more personal and people-centric?

3. Which of the Ten Commandments of Technology and Team (above) is most relevant for your ministry situation?

4. What are a couple of tech rules that would help your team meetings be more effective?

epilogue

BRINGING YOUR SOUL
BACK TO LIFE

M aybe right now you're at a ministry crossroads. Perhaps ministry
and life haven't turned out like you'd hoped. Maybe today you
find yourself empty and drained from the demands of ministry.

There is hope. There is a different way . . . a better way. Your
outward circumstances might not change, but you can change the
trajectory of your soul. With God's help, you really can bring your
soul back to life. Joy can return. Passion can be reignited. Intimacy
can be restored.

Jeremiah has given me a bit of a roadmap on my journey back
to spiritual health.

> This is what the LORD says:
>> "Stand at the crossroads and look;
>> ask for the ancient paths,
>> ask where the good way is, and walk in it,
>> and you will find rest for your souls."[1]

Stand at the crossroads and look.

If you're going to take the road that leads to spiritual health, you have to stand. You have to stop running long enough to make an informed decision about which road you will travel. An old Chinese proverb says, "If we don't change the direction we're going, we're likely to end up where we are headed." Look ahead. If you stay on the road you're traveling today, where are you going to end up?

Ask for the ancient paths. The past is a friend. Many people have walked the road before us, and we can learn a lot from them. This book isn't about new but rather ancient revelation. It's about following the footsteps of those who've gone before us. They're up ahead, motioning back to us and saying, "Come this way. This is the path of spiritual health. This road will help you stay in love with Jesus and finish well."

Ask where the good way is, and walk in it. It's not the fast way. It's not the busy way. It's not even the leadership way that Jeremiah tells us to ask for. It is the good way. God wants you to have a "good" life—a life that is emotionally healthy, relationally satisfying, and spiritually life-giving.

And you will find rest for your souls. What an incredible promise. So many of us in ministry are in need of rest for our soul. Could it be that this is what I really need most and even most deeply long for? Could it be God's first priority in my life is a connected and joyful and refreshed soul? Could it be true in my ministry that his "yoke is easy and [his] burden is light"?[2] Could it be possible to find the kind of rest for my soul that leads me to say, genuinely, "Jesus is enough"?

NOTES

Preface
1. 2 Corinthians 7:1 NLT

Chapter 1: *The Idolatry of Leadership*
1. See Numbers 21:6–9.
2. See 2 Kings 18:4.
3. Research compiled from The Barna Group, Focus on the Family, Fuller Seminary, and the Institute of Church Leadership Development.
4. Parker Palmer, "A Leader Is a Person," *Leading from Within: Reflections on Spirituality and Leadership*, address given at Annual Celebration Dinner of the Indiana Office of Campus Ministries, March 1990.
5. Exodus 28:2
6. Exodus 28:40

Chapter 2: *Hole in My Soul*
1. Ruth Haley Barton, *Strengthening the Soul of Your Leadership: Seeking God in the Crucible of Ministry* (Downers Grove, IL: InterVarsity, 2008), 13.
2. Ibid., 26

3. Gary L. MacIntosh and Samuel D. Rima, *Overcoming the Dark Side of Leadership: How to Become an Effective Leader by Confronting Potential Failures* (Grand Rapids, MI: Baker, 2007, rev. ed.), 27.

4. Henri J. M. Nouwen, *In the Name of Jesus: Reflections on Christian Leadership* (New York: Crossroad, 1989), 29–30.

Chapter 3: *Your Ministry Is Not Your Life*

1. Colossians 3:4
2. Malachi 1:13
3. Exodus 3:11
4. Exodus 32:16
5. Exodus 33:3
6. Exodus 33:15
7. Numbers 12:8
8. Exodus 33:12–13
9. John 15:5 NLT
10. 1 Corinthians 4:20 NLT

Chapter 4: *Image Management*

1. Matthew 23:5 NLT

Chapter 5: *Seduction of Ambition*

1. Ronald Rolheiser, *The Holy Longing: The Search for a Christian Spirituality* (New York: Doubleday, 1999), 14.
2. Ibid., 9.
3. Proverbs 27:21 NLT

Chapter 6: *Ambition Ambush*

1. François Fénelon, *The Seeking Heart* (Jacksonville: Seedsowers, 1992), 147.
2. Thomas Kelly, *A Testament of Devotion* (New York: HarperOne, 1996), 35.
3. James 3:16 NLT
4. Fénelon, *The Seeking Heart*, 41.
5. Andrew Murray, *Humility* (Old Tappan, NJ: Fleming H. Revell, 1961), 45.
6. 1 Peter 5:5–6 NLT

Chapter 8: *Isolation Trap*

1. John C. Maxwell, *Leadership Gold: Lessons I've Learned From a Lifetime of Reading* (Nashville: Thomas Nelson, 2008), 15.
2. Proverbs 11:14 NLT
3. Proverbs 15:31
4. Proverbs 24:26 NLT

Chapter 9: *Need for Speed*
1. James Gleick, *Faster: The Acceleration of Just About Everything* (New York: Vintage Books, 2000), 12.
2. John Ortberg, at a conference.
3. Kelly, *A Testament of Devotion*, 73.

Chapter 10: *Fatigued, Frazzled, and Fried*
1. See Luke 10:40–42.
2. Wayne Cordeiro, *Leading on Empty: Refilling Your Tank and Renewing Your Passion* (Minneapolis: Bethany House, 2009), 21.
3. *Jurassic Park*. Universal Pictures, 1993. Steven Spielberg, Director. Screenplay by Michael Crichton.
4. *Network*. MGM/United Artists, 1976. Sidney Lumet, Director. Written by Paddy Chayefsky.

Chapter 11: *It's Not All About the Weekend*
1. 1 Corinthians 3:13

Chapter 12: *Pit Stops Required*
1. Proverbs 14:8
2. Henry Cloud, *9 Things You Simply Must Do to Succeed in Love and Life* (Nashville: Thomas Nelson, 2004), 72.
3. Andy Stanley, *The Principle of the Path: How to Get from Where You Are to Where You Want to Be* (Nashville: Thomas Nelson, 2008), 14.
4. Ruth Haley Barton, "A Steady Rhythm: The Not-So-Secret Key to Effective Ministry and Leadership" in *Leadership Journal* (Winter 2007). *http://www.christianitytoday.com/le/2007/winter/11.100.html*.

Chapter 13: *What Kind of Old Person Do I Want to Be?*
1. See Joshua 14:14.
2. Gordon MacDonald, *The Life God Blesses: Weathering the Storms of Life That Threaten the Soul* (Nashville: Thomas Nelson, 1994), 98.
3. Nouwen, *In the Name of Jesus*, 10.

Chapter 14: *It's All About the Groom*
1. Revelation 19:7
2. Revelation 19:9
3. John 3:29
4. John 17:24 NLT
5. John Piper, *Seeing and Savoring Jesus Christ* (Wheaton, IL: Crossway, 2004), 21.

Chapter 15: *The Call No One Wants to Get*
1. See Acts 17:6 KJV.

2. Hebrews 11:38
3. Hebrews 11:39
4. Alicia Britt Chole, *Anonymous: Jesus' Hidden Years ... and Yours* (Nashville: Thomas Nelson, 2006), 13.
5. Ibid., 8.
6. Basilea Schlink, *I Found the Key to the Heart of God: My Personal Story* (Minneapolis: Bethany House, 1975), 47–48.

Chapter 16: *Simplicity Is Not Simple*
1. Charles Wagner, *The Simple Life* (Whitefish, MT: Kessinger, 2007), xxxvii.
2. Mindy Caliguire, *Simplicity* (Downers Grove, IL: IVP Connect, 2008), 19.
3. *http://fiveguys.com/faq.aspx*

Chapter 17: *Feel the Rhythm*
1. Barton, *Strengthening the Soul of Your Leadership*, 33.
2. From Noah benShea, *Jacob the Baker: Wisdom for the Heart's Ascent* (New York: Ballantine, 1998), cited in Cordeiro, *Leading on Empty*, 123.
3. Mark 6:31 ISV

Chapter 18: *iPhones and Your Soul*
1. Henri J. M. Nouwen, *With Open Hands* (Notre Dame, IN: Ave Maria, 1972), 36.

Chapter 19: *70% of Pastors Don't Have One*
1. Nouwen, *In the Name of Jesus*, 60.
2. Joseph R. Myers, *The Search to Belong: Rethinking Intimacy, Community, and Small Groups* (Grand Rapids, MI: Zondervan/Youth Specialties, 2003).
3. 1 Samuel 18:3–4 NLT
4. Donald Miller, *A Million Miles in a Thousand Years: What I Learned While Editing My Life* (Nashville: Thomas Nelson, 2009), 228.

Chapter 20: *Identity Theft*
1. Matthew 3:17
2. Chole, *Anonymous*, 41.
3. 1 John 3:1 NLT
4. Galatians 4:7 NLT
5. Psalm 16:5–6

Chapter 21: *Death to Dancing Bears*
1. Eugene H. Peterson, *Under the Unpredictable Plant: An Exploration in Vocational Holiness* (Grand Rapids, MI: Eerdmans, 1994), 16.

2. Richard Baxter, *Watch Your Walk: Ministering From a Heart of Integrity* (Colorado Springs: Victor, 1985), 53.

Chapter 22: *Does Your Soul Have a Backbone?*
1. Deuteronomy 34:12
2. Erwin Raphael McManus, *Uprising: A Revolution of the Soul* (Nashville: Thomas Nelson, 2003), 89.
3. Ambrose Redmoon, "No Peaceful Warrior" in *Gnosis: A Journal of the Western Inner Traditions* (Fall 1991): 21.
4. Martin Luther King Jr., "Our God is Able" in *Strength to Love* (Philadelphia: Fortress, 1963), 113–114.
5. See John 15.
6. Romans 12:17
7. McManus, *Uprising*, 101.
8. 1 Corinthians 16:13 NLT

Chapter 23: *The Art of Doing Nothing*
1. See Leviticus 19:19.
2. See Genesis 2.
3. Lynne M. Baab, *Sabbath Keeping: Finding Freedom in the Rhythms of Rest* (Downers Grove, IL: InterVarsity, 2005), 35.
4. Wayne Muller, *A Life of Being, Having and Doing Enough* (New York: Harmony, 2010), 3.
5. E.g., see at *http://newlifefellowship.org/learning/sabbath-resources/*
6. See NLT.
7. See Exodus 20.

Chapter 24: *Say Yes by Saying No*
1. Barry Schwarz, *The Paradox of Choice: Why More Is Less* (New York: Harper Perennial, 2004), 9.
2. William Ury, *The Power of a Positive No: Save the Deal, Save the Relationship—and Still Say No* (New York: Bantam, 2007), 2.
3. See Mark 1.
4. See Luke 4.
5. Ury, *The Power of a Positive No*, 39.

Chapter 25: *Noise-Canceling Headphones for the Soul*
1. See Exodus 24:16.
2. Mark 1:32–33
3. Mark 1:35
4. Thomas Moore, *Care of the Soul: A Guide for Cultivating Depth and Sacredness in Everyday Life* (New York: HarperCollins, 1992), 286.

5. Gary Thomas, *Seeking the Face of God: A Path to a More Intimate Relationship* (Eugene, OR: Harvest House, 1994), 107.
6. Henri J. M. Nouwen, *The Way of the Heart* (San Francisco: Harper, 1981), 32.
7. Henri J. M. Nouwen, *Out of Solitude: Three Meditations on the Christian Life* (Notre Dame, IN: Ave Maria, 1974), 14.
8. Psalm 131:1–2

Chapter 26: *The Most Embarrassing Gap in My Leadership*
1. My paraphrase; see Mark 11.
2. Mark 11:16
3. Mark 11:17, quoting Isaiah 56:7
4. Proverbs 13:20

Chapter 27: *Humility and Hubris*
1. Andrew Murray, *Humility* (Old Tappan, NJ: Fleming H. Revell, 1961), 18.
2. Matthew 11:29
3. Jim Collins, *How the Mighty Fall: And Why Some Companies Never Give In* (New York: HarperCollins, 2009), 21.
4. John 3:30
5. Proverbs 27:2

Chapter 28: *Stay in Touch With Your Dark Side*
1. See Deuteronomy 5:15, 15:15, 16:12, 24:18, 24:22.
2. Deuteronomy 9:7
3. Isaiah 6:5
4. Fénelon, *The Seeking Heart*, 141.

Chapter 29: *A Valuable Lesson From Alcoholics Anonymous*
1. Resolution 24
2. Steven J. Lawson, *The Unwavering Resolve of Jonathan Edwards* (Orlando: Reformation Trust, 2008), 84.
3. John Baker, *Life's Healing Choices: Freedom from Your Hurts, Hang-ups, and Habits* (New York: Howard, 2007), 106.
4. Jeremiah 17:9
5. Fénelon, *The Seeking Heart*, 10.
6. Proverbs 20:27
7. Psalm 139:23–24 NLT

Chapter 30: *Practicing the Presence of People*
1. Exodus 28:29–30
2. Philippians 1:7 NLT

Chapter 31: *Paying Attention*
1. Numbers 6:24–26
2. Luke 13:12

Chapter 32: *Shock Absorbers for the Soul*
1. Matthew 12:19–20 NLT
2. Bill Hybels, *Axiom: Powerful Leadership Proverbs* (Grand Rapids, MI: Zondervan, 2008), 96.
3. Matthew 11:28–29
4. 1 Timothy 3:3
5. 1 Timothy 6:11
6. 1 Thessalonians 2:7
7. Philippians 4:5

Chapter 33: *The Blessing of Voice and the Voice of Blessing*
1. Proverbs 18:21, my paraphrase
2. See Luke 13.
3. 1 Thessalonians 5:11
4. Luke 24:51

Chapter 34: *The Gift of Loitering*
1. 1 Chronicles 16:12 NLT
2. Psalm 63:3 NLT
3. Psalm 143:5 NLT
4. Philippians 1:3 NLT

Chapter 35: *"Team" Doesn't Have an "I," But It Does Have a "YOU"*
1. Steve Saccone, *Relational Intelligence: How Leaders Can Expand Their Influence Through a New Way of Being Smart* (San Francisco: Jossey-Bass, 2009), 174.

Chapter 36: *Is Your Team Culture More Corporate Than Christlike?*
1. 1 Thessalonians 2:11–12
2. 1 Thessalonians 2:8
3. 1 Thessalonians 2:19–20

Chapter 37: *Speak the Unspoken Rules*
1. Will Mancini, *Church Unique: How Missional Leaders Cast Vision, Capture Culture, and Create Movement* (San Francisco: Jossey-Bass, 2008), 54.
2. Marcus Buckingham, *The One Thing You Need to Know . . . About Great Management, Great Leading, and Sustained Individual Success* (New York: Free Press, 2005), 145–146.

Chapter 38: *Show Up and Speak Up*

1. Susan Scott, *Fierce Conversations: Achieving Success at Work and in Life One Conversation at a Time* (New York: Berkley, 2002), xiii-xiv.
2. Patrick Lencioni, *The Five Dysfunctions of a Team: A Leadership Fable* (San Francisco: Jossey-Bass, 2002), 188.
3. Proverbs 24:26 NLT

Chapter 39: *Are Your Systems Vitamins or Toxins?*

1. Exodus 18:23

Chapter 40: *Going Beyond Alignment to Attunement*

1. D. Michael Abrashoff, *It's Your Ship* (New York: Warner, 2002), 18.
2. Tom Rath and Donald O. Clifton, *How Full Is Your Bucket? Positive Strategies for Work and Life* (New York: Gallup, 2004), 31.
3. Ibid., 39.

Chapter 41: *Ten Commandments of Technology and Team*

1. Vince Poscente, *The Age of Speed: Learning to Thrive in a More-Faster-Now World* (New York: Ballantine, 2008).
2. Ibid., 8.

Epilogue: *Bringing Your Soul Back to Life*

1. Jeremiah 6:16
2. Matthew 11:30

Lance Witt is the founder of REPLENISH (*www.replenish.net*), a ministry dedicated to helping those in Christian leadership live spiritually healthy lives and build spiritually healthy teams.

Lance served twenty years as a senior pastor before serving six years as an executive/teaching pastor at Saddleback Church in Southern California. He led Saddleback's Spiritual Growth Campaigns, including 40 Days of Purpose and 40 Days of Community. He also developed the training tools and resources thousands of churches used in their own implementation of these campaigns. He has spoken at conferences nationally and internationally on topics such as Soul Care, Leadership, Small Groups, and Preaching. Lance has an MDiv from Criswell Seminary and a DMin from Denver Seminary. He has been married to his wife, Connie, for thirty-two years, and they have two married children.

REPLENISH
CURRICULUM

EVERY LEADER FUNCTIONS ON TWO STAGES—

the front stage and the back stage. The front stage is the public world of leadership. The back stage is the private world of the leader. There are many resources to help you succeed on the front stage. But who is talking to you about you and your backstage life?

Together with Lance Witt, Willow Creek Association has created a Replenish Participant Guide and DVD. The Replenish curriculum will provide your team an opportunity to work through 6 sessions that will:

- address problems that lead to burnout
- prioritize matters of the soul
- develop healthy spiritual practices
- create a healthy rhythm in your life
- craft a healthy leadership culture
- develop better systems in your church
- move toward an unhurried life

FOR MORE INFORMATION:
willowcreek.com/
ReplenishCurriculum

Who is talking to you...about YOU?

If you and your team could use some help developing healthy lives and a healthy leadership culture, Replenish would be honored to partner with you.

We can provide...

 Personal Life Coaching

 Team Development

Organizational Consulting

If you would like to explore how Replenish might help you and your team, contact us at
info@replenish.net